Sound Recording for
Motion Pictu

Charles B. Frater

THE TANTIVY PRESS, LONDON
A. S. BARNES & CO., NEW YORK

© 1979 by A. S. Barnes and Co., Inc.

A. S. Barnes and Co., Inc.
Cranbury, New Jersey 08512

The Tantivy Press
Magdalen House
136–148 Tooley Street
London SE1 2TT, England

Library of Congress Cataloging in Publication Data
Frater, Charles.
　　Sound recording for motion pictures.
　　　1. Moving-pictures, Talking. 2. Sound—Recording
and reproducing. I. Title.
TR897.F67　　　778.5′344　　　74-19811
ISBN 0-498-01666-8

In the same
Screen Textbook Series
produced by The Tantivy Press

Compiled and edited by Russell Campbell

Photographic Theory for the Motion Picture Cameraman

Practical Motion Picture Photography

Compiled and edited by Terence St. John Marner

Directing Motion Pictures

Film Design

Printed in the United States of America

Contents

	Introduction	7
I.	Sound Waves	9
II.	Electricity	21
III.	The Sound Recordist's Basic Kit	30
IV.	Synchronous Sound Recording	91
V.	Transfer from Tape to Film	117
VI.	Editing Sound	124
VII.	The Dubbing Theatre	130
VIII.	Preparing a Film for Dubbing	148
IX.	Optical Sound Transfer	163
X.	Recording	171
XI.	Latest Developments	178
	Appendix One: The Nagra III	180
	Appendix Two: The Nagra IV	187
	Appendix Three: The Nagra IS	196
	Appendix Four: The Nagra SN	201
	Appendix Five: Interlock Systems	204
	Appendix Six: Filming to Playback	206
	Index	209

Acknowledgments

One way and another a lot of people have helped me to write this book. I particularly want to thank Miles Smith-Morris for his patience in his dealings with me. He has had to put up with my laziness and the pressures of schedules—a thankless task. Peter Cowie gave me the initial encouragement and impetus to get this project under way. Edward Smith-Morris and Robert Dunbar, who both read the manuscript in its early stages, gave me useful guidelines about its validity as an educational medium. John Colomb, of Better Sound Limited in London, took it on holiday with him to Yugoslavia and, finding that it was the only English reading that he could lay his hands on, gave me invaluable advice on the technical content.

I would like to thank Ted Ryan and Mercury Studio Sound for their advice about dubbing theatres and for allowing me to take photographs of the equipment there. Also my thanks to: Audio Engineering Limited of London for supplying photographs and advice on Crystamatic and Micron Radio Mikes, Hayden Laboratories for help with Nagra equipment and Jim Warren of Miniflux for his help with recording characteristics. Photographs come from the following sources: Levell Electronics Ltd., Klark-Teknik Research Ltd., Grampian Reproducers Ltd., Scopex Instruments Ltd., Acmade, P.A.G. Ltd., John Dixon, J. L. Fisher, Miniflux, Hampstead High Fidelity Ltd., and Rupert Neve and Company Ltd; the table on page 17 contains material from BS 3383: 1961 and is reproduced by permission of BSI, 2 Park Street, London W1A 2BS, from whom complete copies can be obtained.

Introduction

Edison, the American inventor, who made the first practical sound recorder, the phonograph, was the first man to attempt to make sound motion pictures. His invention of the Cinematograph did not stem from a desire to make a moving-picture apparatus, but from the desire to illustrate the sound from the phonograph. In fact his first attempts at motion pictures were built around the phonograph. When these proved impractical he turned to celluloid. Thus in the latter years of the last century sound came first. Today sound is considered as secondary to picture by many people; I think that this is the result more of our automatic perception of sound than of any intent. All the time, night and day, our ears function. The alarm clock wakes us in the morning, the tone of a voice on the telephone increases the flow of adrenalin, we know of the presence of potential danger before a car appears around a corner and curse the jet aeroplane which we cannot see but must hear. The eyes perform in a different way, for one thing we can only look in one direction at a time. At night our eyes are closed and vision replaced by dreams, the ears continue to operate alongside the dreams. Our use of the sense of hearing tends to be automatic; the sound recordist has to develop the sense of hearing so that it is no longer automatic but specific and controlled, the ears have to be used objectively and not subjectively.

Edison's invention of the phonograph was a miracle to the people of the time. Its mechanical simplicity has been replaced by the complexity of the electronic revolution that we are living through. The result of this revolution is an ever increasing ability to reproduce accurately the sounds that we hear. New equipment is continually being designed. Strangely, the techniques for using the equipment do not change much. Rather, it is the things that you can do with the new equipment that makes its arrival interesting. It is not my intention in this book to cover the latest techniques, or to predict the future, but to try to reveal some of the methods and techniques that apply to the equipment that is most commonly in use in the film industry. My personal attitude about sound recording is that the sound recordist is a person who knows how to use the equipment, what equipment to use in a certain circumstance, and above all knows how to use his sense of hearing. I cannot hope to tell the reader how to use his or her ears; this can only be learned by experience in the presence of others who know, and by many many hours and days of listening.

It is therefore a book about the equipment in use to-day, and how it is used.

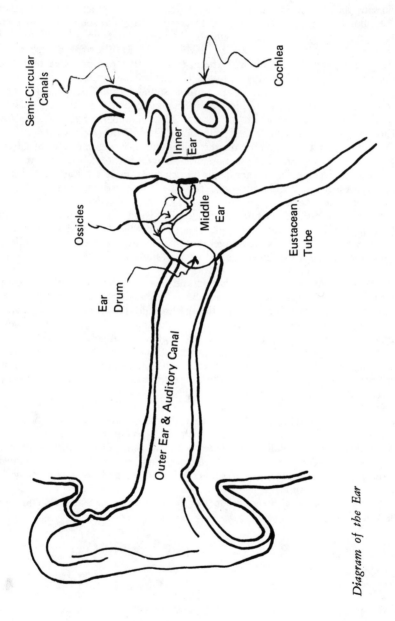

Semi-Circular Canals

Cochlea

Inner Ear

Ossicles

Middle Ear

Eustacean Tube

Ear Drum

Outer Ear & Auditory Canal

Diagram of the Ear

Chapter I

Sound Waves

The air we breathe also provides us with a medium for communication. The vocal chords and the mouth can modulate the medium, the atmosphere, with information, speech. The atmosphere transmits the speech in the form of sound waves which can be received by a suitable sensing organ, the ear. In sound recording we make use of these facts and in equipment like the microphone there is a parallel to the ear in both construction and purpose.

The ear consists of three main sections, the *outer ear*, the *middle ear*, and the *inner ear*. Each section is separated by a thin membrane called a *diaphragm*, the one separating the outer and middle ears being the most important. The outer ear is connected to the inner ear by three small bones which transmit information between the two sections. The diaphragm at the inner end of the outer ear is in direct contact with the atmosphere, and although stretched tight it is flexible, so that any changes in atmospheric pressure make it move in and out depending on whether there is an increase or decrease in pressure. These small movements are transmitted to the inner ear by the three small bones, the *hammer,* the *anvil* and the *stirrup*. The inner ear contains a tube wrapped in an ever-decreasing spiral (like a seashell) which is filled with a liquid and lined with fine hairs; the movements of the diaphragm set the liquid in motion thus stimulating the hairs and the nerve endings which they are connected to. Thus, changes in the atmospheric pressure are converted to nerve impulses and are transmitted to the brain to become the sense which we call hearing.

The middle ear is important as a pressure buffer between the outer and inner ear. It must however maintain its pressure about equal to the mean atmospheric pressure if damage to the diaphragm is to be avoided. This is done by a connecting tube to the atmosphere which runs from the middle ear to the nose—the *eustachian tube*. When this tube is blocked by the effects of a bad cold we sometimes suffer pain caused by the differential in pressure between the atmosphere and the middle ear and only by clearing the tube can we get rid of the pain.

The nerve endings connected to the hairs in the inner ear are very sensitive and may be easily damaged by excessive exposure to noise. As a measure of the sensitivity it is interesting to note that they are not provided with a blood supply since this would subject the listener to a constant thumping sound from the heartbeats which would make all other sounds inaudible. Interesting too, to note, that the eye has similarly a part which is blood free, the cornea.

When we speak we modulate the air leaving our lungs with our vocal chords; in other words the smooth flow of air through the wind pipe is interrupted rapidly, and instead of leaving the mouth smoothly, it comes out in a series of puffs which are further varied by the mouth itself. These rapid variations change the pressure of the atmosphere very slightly, but enough to stimulate the diaphragm of an ear within a reasonable distance. The medium, in this case the atmosphere, but it could be water or, with appropriate equipment, the ether, a gramophone record, a tape, a film, or a laser beam, has been modulated from its steady state into one which carries information. The ear, constructed as it is to accept information relating to changes in atmospheric pressure, responds to voice modulations and we perceive sound. A piece of paper held in front of the mouth while speaking will vibrate, and thus it will be seen that sound waves can be perceived by the sense of touch (although not perhaps understood).

In technical terms the vocal chords and the ear are known as *transducers,* devices which change one medium into another. The vocal chords take an air-stream and modulate it while the ear transforms the atmospheric pressure changes into nerve impulses. Other devices, like the microphone and the loudspeaker, the TV camera, the pickup in a gramophone, etc, are all transducers.

The *medium* carries or stores the information. The *transducers* encode, and transmit the information and then decode it at the receiving end.

The next thing to examine is how the atmosphere carries sound, and what exactly sound is. Radio waves and light are an electro-magnetic effect, the transmission of sound through the atmosphere is mechanical. The pressure of the atmosphere is roughly constant from moment to moment, although of course large variations take place as a result of changes in the weather, but the ear is not sensitive to such slow variations. In fact the lowest rate of change of pressure which the ear will turn into nerve impulses is about twenty complete variations per second. Not only does the pressure in the atmosphere remain roughly constant but it tries to maintain a constant pressure. The molecules of nitrogen, oxygen, and carbon dioxide which make up the atmosphere are part of a gas and are in constant motion, each reacting upon the next. If the pressure increases, the molecules are pressed closer together, and assuming that the gas is contained in a limited space, if the pressure increases in one part of the space the tendency will be for the pressure to equalise throughout that space; thus, the increased pressure is transmitted from one molecule to the next. This mechanical transmission of pressure is slow, an effect exaggerated by the elasticity of the medium. The reverse, of course, applies when the pressure is reduced; molecules rush in to try to fill the space, and the attempt is made to try to equalise the pressure. This is the basis of the sound wave.

We have already seen that the ear will not accept variations in atmospheric pressure of less than about twenty per second, therefore the almost static situation of a single sudden pressure change is not valid. However if the pressure changes rapidly in the atmosphere with a cyclic action of increases and decreases in pressure a sound exists. In this situation it is obvious that there will not be enough time for the pressure of the whole environment to equalise. Assuming then that the source of pressure change is small, waves of high and low pressure will leave the source. In effect there will be small movements of the molecules in the atmosphere as they move back and forth in their attempts to bring the pressure to a point of equilibrium. The movement of these waves from the source of sound is, as already mentioned, comparatively slow, about 1100ft (335m) per second, the speed of sound. This speed is varied by the atmospheric conditions prevailing at the time.

When the vocal chords and the mouth vary the rate at which the air leaves the lungs, in effect they are varying the atmospheric pressure very slightly. Radiating from the mouth are sound waves consisting of zones of high and low pressure following each other in rapid succession.

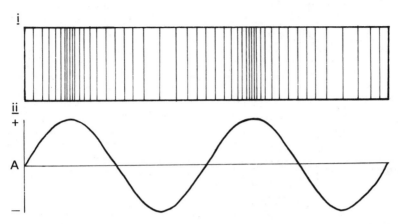

(i) Cross-section showing compression and rarefaction of the molecules in the atmosphere caused by a sound wave. (ii) shows how this can be resolved graphically. A = normal atmospheric pressure and the + and — signs the increases and decreases in pressure around this point.

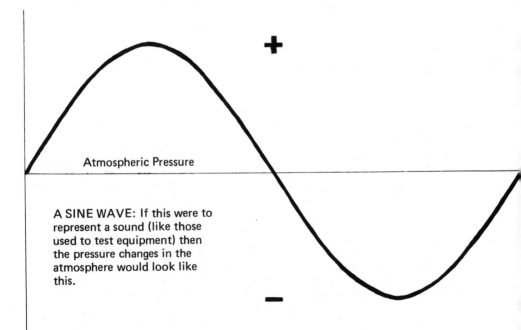

+

Atmospheric Pressure

A SINE WAVE: If this were to represent a sound (like those used to test equipment) then the pressure changes in the atmosphere would look like this.

—

Sound waves are not like the waves in the ocean which to all intents and purposes are two-dimensional. Sound waves are three-dimensional. However we tend to illustrate them graphically, with a result which looks like a section through a sea wave, and there could be confusion. The simplest and most economical sound wave is the *sine wave,* so called because it is derived mathematically. It appears again and again in discussion about sound, and is used extensively in testing and setting up sound equipment. Since it is simple, it is easy to understand.

Firstly, the atmospheric pressure changes that it represents are cyclic; they repeat themselves uniformly in time. The line in the graph represents the changes in atmospheric pressure about the norm. A complete cycle is one in which the pressure is changed from the norm through the maximum, through the norm, and through the minimum back to the norm again, to the point at which the whole process is about to start again. If there was one complete cycle in a second then the dimensions of the sound wave would be equal to the distance travelled by sound waves in one second, 1100ft (335m). Two cycles per second would halve the *wavelength,* 550 ft (167.5m). The formula for establishing the wavelength of a sound wave is:

$$\frac{\text{SPEED OF SOUND}}{\text{FREQUENCY}} = \lambda \, (\text{wavelength})$$

Frequency is the number of complete cycles in a second, and is measured in *hertz* (Hz).

2 cycles per second (cps) = 2 Hertz (Hz)
1000 cps (1 Kilocycle/1Kc) = 1000 Hz (1 KHz)

There are many who still talk of cycles per second, but Hertz has the advantage that it is an international standard and is understood by everybody.

WAVELENGTH

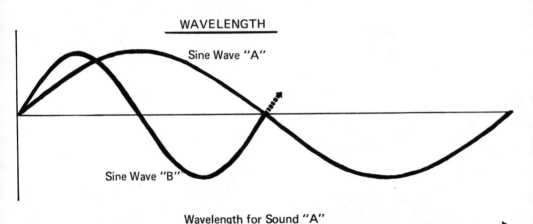

Sine Wave "A"

Sine Wave "B"

Wavelength for Sound "A"

If this was the distance the sound traveled in one second, the sound would have a frequency of one cycle per second (1Hz)

Sound "B" has half the wavelength of "A". It is therefore possible to cram 2 complete cycles into the same time (the speed of sound being constant for given circumstances) and it has a frequency of two cycles per second (2 Hz)

Wavelength, frequency and the speed of sound are three dimensions of the sound wave which are related to time. The frequency spectrum of sound waves is considerable. For sound recording it is only necessary to be involved with those frequencies which can be perceived by the ear. As has been seen the ear begins to hear at about 20Hz; there is a certain amount of doubt about whether the ear actually hears such a low frequency, or whether the body itself 'feels' the sound. Certainly at a frequency of 30Hz we can hear. The upper limit of hearing lies between 15KHz and 20KHz, and differs with the individual and age, response to high frequencies deteriorating with increasing age.

Pitch, a musical term, is directly related to frequency. The standard musical note used by the orchestra is A′, which has a frequency of 440Hz, and indeed it is not unusual for the orchestra to get aid from electronic tone generators to help them tune to the standard. The octave above the standard A′ has a frequency of 880Hz, i.e. double. If the frequency of a note is doubled, it sounds twice as high, and is an octave higher, and vice versa. The musical notes between the two notes which constitute an octave have a definite pattern which can be worked out mathematically. A string vibrating at 440Hz, as in a piano or violin, can also vibrate at double the frequency, and also at treble the frequency, etc. In certain circumstances it is possible to hear all three notes at the same time; the bottom note, 440Hz, is called the *fundamental,* the others are called the second and third *harmonics* respectively. By adding the fundamental and the second harmonic together as in the graph (see below) it can be seen that the two can be resolved together to produce a new wave-form which is no longer sinusoidal, the same could be done with the third harmonic. In this way it is possible for the violin string to produce three sounds at the same time and for the single sound wave emanating therefrom to carry the sound. Most sounds are incredibly complex combinations of harmonics with the fundamental and the 3rd, 4th, 5th, etc harmonics. The third harmonic has a frequency 3 times that of the fundamental, the fourth harmonic 4 times that of the fundamental etc.

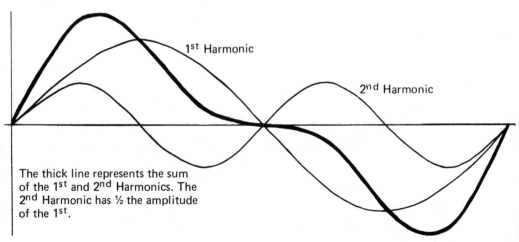

1st Harmonic

2nd Harmonic

The thick line represents the sum of the 1st and 2nd Harmonics. The 2nd Harmonic has ½ the amplitude of the 1st.

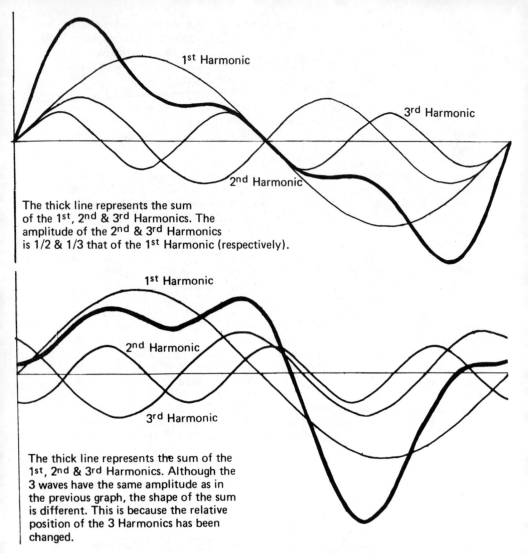

1st Harmonic

3rd Harmonic

2nd Harmonic

The thick line represents the sum
of the 1st, 2nd & 3rd Harmonics. The
amplitude of the 2nd & 3rd Harmonics
is 1/2 & 1/3 that of the 1st Harmonic (respectively).

1st Harmonic

2nd Harmonic

3rd Harmonic

The thick line represents the sum of the
1st, 2nd & 3rd Harmonics. Although the
3 waves have the same amplitude as in
the previous graph, the shape of the sum
is different. This is because the relative
position of the 3 Harmonics has been
changed.

Musical instruments get their tone from the proportion of harmonics
the sound they make contains. Thus the violin can be mellow, when the
violinist wishes, being played in such a way that the lower harmonics pre-
dominate, and harsh when the higher harmonics are emphasised. The relative
strengths of the harmonics help us to differentiate between the violin, the
viola, the French horn and the oboe. The other difference between instruments lies in the way the sounds they make begin and end. Thus the violin
does not sound very much like the piano, which although it is a stringed
instrument is also a percussion instrument. The sound from a piano is very
strong to begin with and then decays very rapidly, whereas the violinist can
keep a note going at a constant rate for quite a time. Attempts to duplicate

the sound of the orchestra in the great Wurlitzer cinema organs of the Twenties and Thirties did not succeed because the proportions of the harmonics and the shape of the notes did not really emulate the instruments of the orchestra. (I do not deny that the sound they made was unique and thrilling in its own right.) The electronic music synthesizer is beginning to be able to produce sounds very similar to those made by instruments in the orchestra. The violin does not rely only on the strings for the sound that it makes. The body of the instrument is extremely important in the design of a violin and indeed defines the cash value, because of the sound made. The sound box, for that is what it is, is connected to the strings by the bridge, the front and back plates are connected together by a post, the sound post. Thus the vibrations of the strings are connected to a large area which radiates the sound and amplifies it. The sound box is a resonator, like a string stretched to a certain tension, the air in an enclosed space with a certain volume will vibrate at a specified frequency, in the violin sound box the number of possibilities is huge since there are a great number of differing distances between the sides. A simpler example, the organ pipe, is designed to resonate at a specific frequency which is defined by the relationship between the length of the pipe and the wavelength of the sound produced. The sound is produced by air blown past a whistle or reed which sets the air in the column vibrating. The pitch of the sound is defined by the length of the tube which may be closed or open at the end. The sound wave in the tube will have a wavelength the same as the length of the tube if it is open, or twice the length of the tube if it is closed since that is the frequency at which the tube will resonate. Of course this will be the fundamental or first harmonic, and it will be possible for harmonics to exist. If a reed is used it will be necessary to adjust its tension so that it will vibrate at or near the frequency of the fundamental or a harmonic. The pipe can be tuned by varying its length; the longer the tube, the longer the wavelength, and, therefore, the lower the frequency. If the tube is closed at the end, sound waves will be reflected back along the tube, and, therefore, pressure waves that have been reflected will meet those coming along the tube. Where they meet there will be what is known as a *nodal* point. *Anti-nodes* are the points at which low pressure and high pressure meet. At nodes the sound is increased in strength, and at anti-nodes the sound is decreased in strength, a definite factor in the design of environments for listening to and recording sound.

Sound waves do not only vary in frequency, wavelength and speed, they also vary in *amplitude* (see illustration), in other words the variation in pressure imposed on the atmosphere by a sound can be small or large. The unit for measuring the relative loudness of a sound is the *decibel* (dB). It has been discovered by experiment that most people when subjected to a sound of one intensity in comparison to another of changing intensity will say that the changing sound is twice as loud when the power of the sound has been

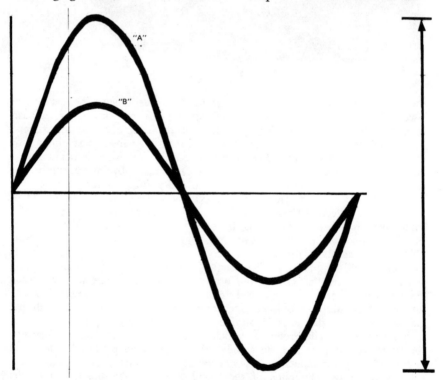

Amplitude: The graph shows two sound waves of the same wavelength (and therefore frequency) but of different amplitude and therefore loudness—A has a greater amplitude than B and is therefore louder.

multiplied by a factor of ten. This phenomenon takes place at all the loudnesses that we can happily perceive. Thus a sound as soft as a whisper when multiplied by ten will sound twice as loud, so too will a loud sound like a clap of thunder. The ratio between two sounds differing in power by a factor of ten was called the *Bel* (after the inventor of the telephone, Alexander Graham Bell), and it was divided by ten to give the more convenient decibel (dB).

Further experiments established that most people with healthy ears start hearing at a certain sound level which was called the *threshold of hearing*. The energy needed to produce a sound at the loudness of the threshold of hearing at 1KHz is very small, being 0.0002 dynes/cm². One has unfortunately to state the frequency at which the measurement is made because the ear is not equally sensitive to all frequencies at the threshold of hearing, as shown by the following curves of equal loudness (sometimes called the Fletcher/ Munsen curves).

At between 125dB and 130dB above the threshold of hearing the point is reached at which the ear begins to experience pain, the *threshold of pain*. This

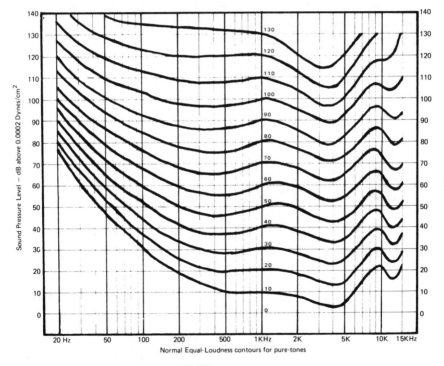

Normal Equal-Loudness contours for pure-tones

Copies (& simplified) from British Standard 3383:1961

This graph illustrates the frequency response of the ear, which is not 'flat' but varies with frequency. For example, a 1KHz tone which is reproduced at a loudness of 70dB above the threshold of hearing sounds 20dB louder than a tone of 40Hz played at the same loudness. This means that 40Hz tone needs to be 20dB louder for it to sound as loud as the 1KHz tone.

17

dB Above Threshold of Hearing	Relative Intensity	Loudness of Familiar Sounds	Comments		
130	10,000,000,000,000	Jet Engines Nearby	Threshold of Pain		
120	1,000,000,000,000				
110	100,000,000,000				
100	10,000,000,000	Loud Orchestra			
90	1,000,000,000	Loud Lorry		Dynamic Range: Orchestra	A Signal to Noise Ratio
80	100,000,000				Orchestra
70	10,000,000				
60	1,000,000	Speech			
50	100,000				
40	10,000				
30	1,000	Audience			
20	100	Single Soft Violin			
10	10				
0	1	0 dB=0.0002 dynes/dm^2 The Threshold of Hearing			

represents a power range for the ear with a factor of 10^{13} or 10,000,000,000,000 times. The accompanying table gives approximate values for some of the sounds we are familiar with. The values vary considerably with environment and distance and should not be regarded as anything more than a guide.

It will be noted that I have not been able to express the threshold of pain as an absolute value in decibels. The decibel expresses a ratio in loudness between two sounds, and therefore the value for the threshold of pain has to be anchored to the threshold of hearing—130dB above the threshold of hearing.

The value of 35dB above the threshold of hearing given for the softest that a single violin can play may perhaps be regarded as the softest note that the orchestra can play. About 70dB above that point the instruments of the orchestra all playing together reach their loudest. This range between the softest and loudest sound for any particular sound is known as the *dynamic range* and is expressed in decibels. Since the decibel expresses a ratio between two sounds this is legitimate.

Unfortunately the audience in a concert hall makes more noise than the single violinist, even when they are sitting quietly. Noise is undesirable sound, usually in competition with desirable sound. The violinist, in an effort to hear himself and make himself heard, makes an automatic adjustment and plays slightly louder. The noise in the concert hall has had the effect of decreasing the dynamic range of the orchestra. In electronic equipment, the ratio between the loudest sound (in technical terms, the *signal*) and the noise is very important, and generally determines the dynamic range of the

18

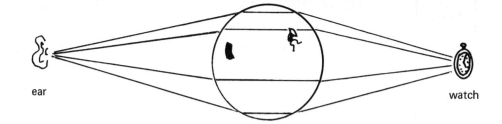

ear

watch

Balloon filled with
carbon dioxide
acting as lens

equipment. This is known as the *signal-to-noise ratio,* and is expressed in decibels.

Sound waves behave much as light waves: they can be bent, reflected and absorbed. A classic experiment is carried out in secondary school science classes of refraction of sound waves. Sound waves reaching a gas-filled balloon are bent (as when light strikes the glass of a prism) and the listener can hear the ticking of a watch loud and clear when his ear is at the focal point.

Huygen's principle states that if parallel sound waves encounter an obstacle in which there is an opening, waves with a wavelength greater than the opening will radiate beyond the obstacle in a way which makes the opening look like a point source of sound, and that if the wavelength of the sound is shorter than the dimensions of the opening, these will continue unaffected. This is important in the design of loudspeakers, since it affects the direction of radiation of sound from the speaker relative to frequency.

The obstacle effect is the reverse of Huygen's principle. It states that sound will be reflected by an obstacle with dimensions greater than the wavelength of the sound. Therefore the brass band which plays in an open field is not subjected to sounds which are reflected; however, in the village square, where the buildings are, on the whole, obstacles with greater dimensions than the sound wavelengths, there will be reflection of sound and consequently echo.

Sound waves can be reflected and absorbed. Reflections take place from hard flat surfaces. An uncarpeted unfurnished room has a dramatic effect on sound which becomes hollow and echoed; fill the room with furnishings and the sound waves will be absorbed to quite a degree. The first room is said to be 'live', and the second 'dead'. This type of qualification is very vague, and the scientists engaged in the study of the behaviour of sound in the environment, *acoustics*, spend much money trying to find objective methods of analysis. A room behaves rather like the closed organ pipe. If the room is similar to a cube then there is a complicated series of reflections. Certain frequencies are emphasised according to the distance between the parallel walls and their relationship to the wavelength of the sounds (so-called *Eigen tones*). In the design of studios this is an important aspect, since it is important to design an environment which is acoustically neutral and does not

19

emphasise specific frequencies through resonance. The walls can be treated so that they do not reflect much sound by coating them with a soft absorbent material, and they can be broken up so that they are not parallel. The design of a studio control room is as important, and there are now specifications available for standard listening rooms which should help to establish control of quality from studio to studio.

The motion-picture sound recordist does not need to concern himself with the details of acoustics. Only the sound that is recorded is important. If, for instance, dialogue is not intelligible because it was recorded in a place with very reflective walls and has therefore too much echo, then the sound recordist has failed, either through not taking appropriate steps while making the recording or not advising against making the recording in that environment at all. If, on the other hand, the picture associated with the sound needed echo, the environment will have been helpful. The sound recordist should be able to recognise the acoustic qualities of a place by its appearance and by the sound of ordinary conversation in it, and by the sounds that he hears arriving at the place from outside its confines. If his analysis of the situation is that a good or appropriate recording cannot be made, he should say so. Only experience can dictate these judgments. Any scientific assessment of acoustics can only be validated by subjective listening tests, and it is therefore the ear and what it hears (and how that information is analysed) that is most important.

Chapter II
Electricity

All modern sound equipment depends to some extent on the properties of electricity. The manipulation of electricity, especially in very small quantities is called *electronics*. It is electronics which most concern us.

The *electron* is a negative particle or charge associated with atomic matter. The *proton* is positive and comparatively massive and together with the *neutron*, which has no charge, makes up most of the mass of the world which surrounds us, and indeed ourselves. The electron is the negative charge which balances the positive charge of the proton in an atom.

In the atmosphere, sound is transmitted not by the bodily movement of large quantities of atoms but by small movements which pass the energy from one atom to the next. Electricity is transmitted down a wire in the same way. Nobody has yet defined the exact nature of electricity; we do know that it is energy, which is easily transmitted by certain materials which are known as conductors. This is done by excitation of the outer shell of electrons surrounding each molecule of the conductor. The excitation of one molecule excites the next one and so on, and in the same way that the atmosphere transmits the mechanical energy of sound waves by the movement of whole atoms, electricity is transmitted through a wire by the movement of the electron shells around the atoms.

There are two main types of electricity: direct current (DC) and alternating current (AC). These terms simply apply to how the electricity moves through the conductor. In direct current this flow is in one direction only, from negative to positive, since electricity is conducted primarily by the excitation or movement of the electron. The speed at which the energy is transmitted through the wire is constant, the intensity (measured in *volts*) and the quantity (measured in *amps*) are variable. The same parameters are applied to alternating current although the system for sending energy along the wire relies on the rapid change in the direction of the flow of electricity.

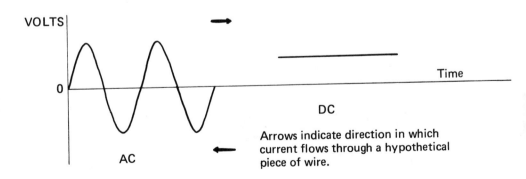

Arrows indicate direction in which current flows through a hypothetical piece of wire.

In most countries in the world the mains electricity is supplied using alternating current which has a frequency of 50Hz, and looks like (indeed is) a sine wave when examined graphically. The United States of America, Canada, parts of Mexico and Japan use a 60Hz mains current.

A battery supplies direct current. Providing there is no connection between the terminals of the battery there is, at the terminals, a potential for producing electricity. This remains until tapped by connecting some device which by its nature draws out the potential energy. A straight piece of wire[1] made

---

[1] If the wire were coiled it would become an inductor, about which more later.

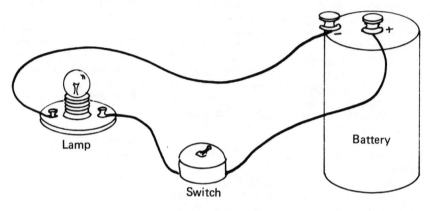

Lamp

Switch

Battery

An Electrical Circuit

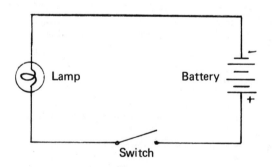

Lamp

Battery

Switch

The equivalent circuit diagram

The circuit illustrated is incomplete until the switch is operated.

from a good conductor like copper will complete the circuit and the full power of the battery will be transmitted by the wire. This assumes that the wire is a good conductor. If it is not it will resist the passage of energy. This resistance has the same effect as the resistance of the brakes of a motor car on the movement of the car and the wire gets hot. In normal circumstances the wire gets so hot that it melts, sometimes so quickly that there is an explosion. If the resistance of the wire is carefully calculated and the wire is contained in a glass envelope filled with an inert gas we have an electric light bulb.

The point about the foregoing is that there has to be a source of electric energy before we can talk about electricity and likewise from the practical point of view there has to be a complete electrical circuit before electricity is of any use to us.

All electrical circuits have a resistance to the flow of electricity. This is called *resistance* and is measured in *ohms*. There is a simple and regular relationship between resistance, voltage and current. (VOLTS = Emf (Electromotive Force), AMPS = I, OHMS = R (Resistance).) The relationship between the three can easily be remembered by the triangle: which starting

at the top is in alphabetical order. The equations for the relationship (known as *Ohm's Law*) are as follows:

$$E = IR$$
$$I = \frac{E}{R}$$
$$R = \frac{E}{I}$$

As formulae these may seem to be unimportant. I certainly thought so at one time. Nevertheless I find that I use them from time to time to make calculations.

The power of a piece of equipment, like an electric lamp, is the product of the intensity of the energy driving it and the amount of energy, i.e. volts × amps, known as VA and as *watts*, the two expressions being slightly different in their meaning.

Ohms as units affect the sound recordist more as units of impedance than as units of resistance. Impedance is the resistance displayed by a circuit to AC. Unfortunately resistance to AC depends on other properties, *inductance* and *capacitance*. It is not within the scope of this book to make a detailed and scientific explanation of these two phenomena, but I hope that a simple one will suffice and make it clear why the sound recordist needs to know a bit about electronic terminology.

A capacitor consists of two plates which are in close proximity and yet insulated from each other. Sometimes the insulator used is paper, and thin paper at that, or in the case of what is called an electrolytic capacitor, a layer of insulation a few molecules thick. This device is used to store small quan-

SYMBOLS FOR CAPACITORS

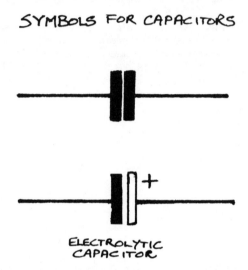

ELECTROLYTIC
CAPACITOR

tities of electricity. What happens is that when a potential is attached to the plates, positive to one side and negative to the other, there is a brief flow of electricity in an attempt to complete the circuit. This cannot happen because of the insulation, but what does happen is that electrons build up on the negative plate of the capacitor and electrons leave the positive plate. The result is known as an *electrostatic charge*—static because there is no circuit and therefore no flow of electricity. There is however a potential—the electrostatic charge—left behind when the original charging force from the battery is removed. Thus, if the capacitor is left in a circuit, it will release its potential and discharge. The capacity for holding a charge is called capacitance and is measured in *Farads*—the common unit being the micro farad: μF. Now it will be seen that if a capacitor is put into a circuit with a battery, i.e. a DC power source, the ultimate resistance of the capacitor to the flow of current is very large and is in fact infinity. But in a situation where the supply of electricity alternates and the current reverses its direction continuously the capacitor charges and discharges at a similar rate. It has, however, to experience some kind of potential difference before it can charge or discharge and therefore will not do so in synchronism with the current which drives the circuit. The rate at which the capacitor will charge and discharge is also dependent on its capacity, so that its resistance to the flow of current will vary according to the frequency of the current.

A coil of wire is said to have inductance. This electrical property is also one which displays resistance to alternating current. To understand why it does this it is necessary to know something about magnetic fields and their effects upon electrical conductors.

When a conductor is passed through a magnetic field there is an interaction between the lines of magnetic force and the electrons in the conductor which create an electric current. The direction and strength of the electric current formed depend on

(a) The direction of movement of the wire and the polarity of the magnetic field.

(b) the intensity of the magnetic field and the speed of movement of the conductor.

There are definite rules which were laid down last century and immortalised in *Fleming's right hand rule.* The opposite applies (leading to *Fleming's left hand rule*). If an electric current is passed through a conductor then a magnetic field is formed, the strength and direction of which is determined by the strength and direction of the electric current.

The use of a single wire as an inductor is inefficient, and the normal practice is to coil the wire on some kind of former. This has the effect of concentrating the magnetic field that surrounds the wire. Furthermore if the core around which the wire is wound is made from a magnetic conductor like

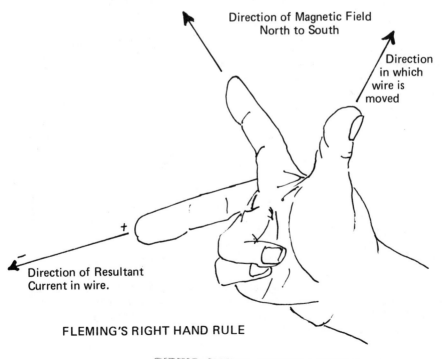

Direction of Magnetic Field
North to South

Direction in which wire is moved

+

Direction of Resultant Current in wire.

FLEMING'S RIGHT HAND RULE

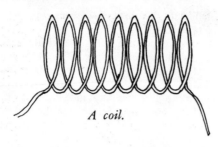

A coil.

Drawing: Sue Chambers.

soft iron then the effect of concentration is increased. A coil of wire is known as an inductor.

As with the capacitor, the inductor displays a resistance to AC which is different to that which it displays to DC.

When a direct current is passed into a coil, there is a fraction in time while the magnetic field is building up to match the size of the current creating it, when there is a greater resistance to the flow of electricity. When the DC is removed the reverse happens. The electric current which is sustaining the magnetic field collapses immediately, but the magnetic field collapses a fraction of a second later. As the lines of magnetic force cut through the wires in the inductor a new electric current is generated. Thus it will be seen that an inductor has a different resistance to DC to that it has to AC.

If a capacitor and an inductor are combined in a circuit their opposite effects can be combined to create resonant circuits which either pass or attenuate alternating currents at specific frequencies (depending on the values selected for the components). This is an extreme example of impedance varying with frequency.

All sound equipment has to deal with alternating current with quite a large range of frequencies, the frequency range of the human ear. All sound equipment therefore has resistance to alternating current: impedance. Fortunately there are some rough standards and facts about impedance which the sound recordist should know and which enable him to match different pieces of equipment without trouble.

(a)   The output impedance of a piece of equipment (amplifier, microphone, turntable cartridge, etc) should be lower than the input impedance of the device into which it is looking.

(b)   The output impedances of microphones are generally 50 or 200 ohms. Amplifiers are designed to accept either one or the other, but in effect the difference is not that great and although not ideal, in an emergency using the wrong mike will do, especially if a 50 ohm mike is used in an input designed to accept a 200 ohm mike. A high impedance mike, of 50 or 100 Kilohms would definitely not be suitable.

(c)   The impedance of the average loudspeaker lies between 4 and 16 ohms.

(d)   The industry standard impedance for the transmission of signals down lines is 600 ohms.

(e)   It is easier to transmit a signal along a long length of cable if the output and input impedances of the equipment used are low (600 ohms or lower). The higher the impedance the shorter the length of cable because of the capacitive effect of the conductors in the cable.

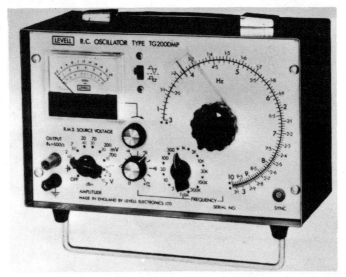

An oscillator designed to produce sine waves from 1Hz to 1KHz.
Photo: Levell Electronics.

Electrical measurements made in the servicing of sound equipment can easily be accomplished with three basic pieces of equipment, the *oscillator,* the *multimeter* (and in certain cases an AC voltmeter which is a meter designed with microvolt sensitivity for the measurement of low AC voltages) and an *oscilloscope* (this last not always by any means being necessary).

An oscillator is an amplifier which makes tone, or sine wave, signals. The output of the device is usually low impedance or 600 ohms, can be varied in voltage from microvolts to volts (thus making it possible to simulate microphone and line sources), and can be varied in frequency from a few hertz to 0.5 or 1 megahertz.

The voltmeter used in conjunction with the oscillator makes it possible to make most of the tests that one needs to do to find out whether a piece of equipment is working properly or not. Let us assume that an amplifier is suspect. The oscillator can be fed into one end of the device while the voltmeter is used to measure the strength of the signal at the output. The output voltage should be constant regardless of frequency over the whole range of frequencies encompassed by the human ear.

The oscillator is built with a much larger frequency range than the ear because it is also used to test items in equipment which have, for instance in the tape recorder, oscillators with an output frequency of anywhere between 50KHz and 150KHz. The frequency of these oscillators can be found out in conjunction with an oscilloscope.

The oscilloscope is a cathode ray tube and associated amplifiers which make it possible to display electrical signals visually. The display is created by a beam of electrons which is focused onto a screen which lights up, as a result of the bombardment, and a dot can be seen. This dot, i.e. the beam of

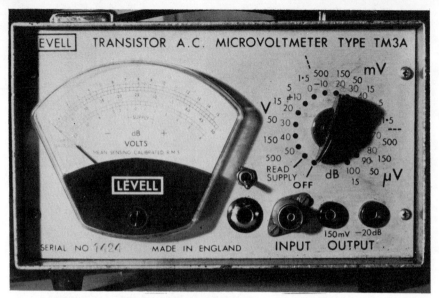

A typical voltmeter used for testing audio equipment. It is capable of measuring very small voltages such as those produced by a microphone.

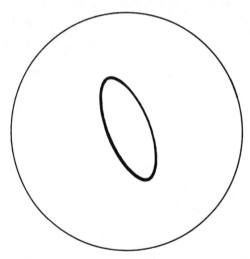

Drawing of a lissajous pattern as it appears on an oscilloscope screen.

electrons viewed end on, is moved from left to right by a scanning amplifier. When the dot has reached the right-hand side of the screen the process is repeated, but during the moment it takes for the dot to return to the left-hand side of the screen it is blanked out so that only the left to right movement is seen. The scanning amplifier can be adjusted so that the number of scans per

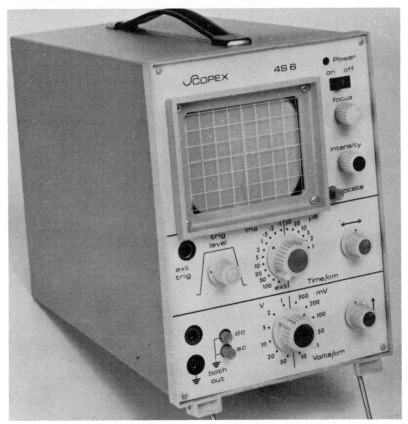

An oscilloscope.   *Photo: Scopex Instruments Ltd.*

second can be varied. So far the dot has only been moved horizontally. The signal which is to be studied is fed into an amplifier which moves the dot vertically. If the frequency of the input signal is the same as that of the horizontal scanning of the dot then the picture will be stationary. If not then the picture wanders to one side or the other. Thus it is crucial to adjust the frequency of the scanning to that of the signal being studied. Alternatively it is possible to trigger the horizontal scan everytime the input signal takes an upward or downward swing. It is also possible to feed a signal into the horizontal axis of the oscilloscope without going through the scanning amplifiers, and another into the vertical axis, forming what is called a *lissajous* pattern if the two frequencies are equal. Thus it is possible to determine the frequency of the oscillator in a tape recorder by comparison with the calibrated frequency obtainable from an oscillator.

The oscillator and AC voltmeter can also be used to determine the signal-to-noise ratio of equipment.

On the whole the sound recordist of to-day does not need to have a great knowledge of the electronics of his equipment. It is useful if he can test a microphone cable, and use a soldering iron to fix it.

Chapter III

The Sound Recordist's Basic Kit

Sound tracks for motion pictures are made in five definite stages with some possible alternative sub-stages. The main stages are *shooting, transfer, editing, mixing,* and *transfer to optical.* To begin with, shooting.

The sound recordist will need to have a basic kit of equipment. In the main this will consist of *microphones, a recorder* and *microphone cables.* There are accessories of one kind or another which are determined by the script and therefore the needs of the film. The sound recordist can go out into the field not knowing anything of how the equipment works, but on the whole it is better to know what is going on in order to be prepared for any problems which may arise. This chapter will therefore examine the basic equipment in the kit.

Firstly, though, it would be a good idea to note these simple rules for the care of sound equipment.

(1) Do not drop.
(2) Keep dry.
(3) When not being used keep it in its box.
(4) Do not expose to extremes of temperature.
(5) Do not run equipment at a voltage greater than that recommended by the manufacturer.

Sound equipment is very reliable and if the above rules are observed will, on the whole, give no trouble.

Microphones:

A microphone is a transducer. A transducer converts one medium of communication into another; for instance, a television camera changes light into an electric signal which can be recorded, altered and manipulated, and then transmitted to another transducer, the TV set, which changes it back into light (the picture). A microphone changes sound waves into electrical energy, which after suitable treatment in an amplifier can be transduced back into sound by a loudspeaker.

The way in which a microphone behaves is both electrical and physical. There are five general properties which we look for:

(1) *Good frequency response.* This means that the microphone must duplicate as nearly as possible in electricity the sound waves which it encounters, and it must do this over the whole range of the ear. So the frequency response must extend from about 20 or 30Hz to 20KHz, and, since we are interested not in reproducing what the ear hears but the sound as it exists in the atmosphere, the microphone must be equally sensitive to sound waves regardless of frequency.

(2) *Low distortion.* Distortion is a widely-used word to describe the difference in the shape and form of a sound wave after it has been manipulated by equipment. A microphone which has an uneven frequency response could

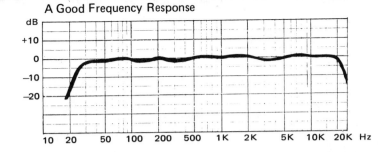

A Good Frequency Response

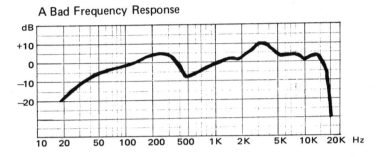

A Bad Frequency Response

be said to be adding distortion. This is not the usual description of distortion. Distortion is something which we can hear and an everyday example is what happens to the sound in a cheap transistorized radio. The sort of distortion which we are worried about in a microphone is in its ability to work in areas of very high noise. A microphone should be able to convert sounds which we would find painful to listen to, into electricity, without distortion. This relates very much to the next quality that we expect from a microphone.

(3) *High signal-to-noise ratio.* The electrical noise present in a microphone should be as low as possible; this means that when recording very soft sounds they will not be masked by the noise of the mike itself. There is obviously a need for the microphone to be sensitive and to produce a reasonable amount of electricity when it is used in areas of soft sound.

(4) *Compatibility with other equipment.* The sensitivity of a microphone has a bearing upon whether it is compatible with other equipment. For instance if a microphone which is very sensitive is fed into a very sensitive tape recorder, the chances are that any sounds louder than speech will drive the recorder into distortion because the voltage from the microphone will be too high for the amplifiers. This is the preferable way round since it is a simple matter to add an attenuator to reduce sensitivity, but not always simple to increase the sensitivity of the equipment. Compatibility of microphones with amplifiers is governed by impedance. This is the electrical resistance of the microphone and the amplifier to alternating current, expressed in ohms. Sound produces an alternating current which varies in frequency in the circuit in sympathy with the frequency of the sound (see Chap. II). What the sound recordist needs to know is the effects of mis-matching impedances between the

31

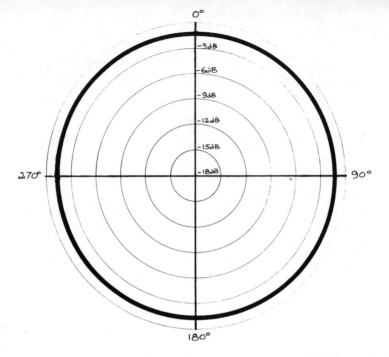

0°
-3dB
-6dB
-9dB
-12dB
-15dB
-18dB
270°
90°
180°

Polar diagrams Above: OMNI-DIRECTIONAL microphone. The sensitivity of the microphone to sounds coming from different directions is equal. Opposite page-top: BI-DIRECTIONAL microphone. The microphone is sensitive to sounds from two directions only. This is typical of ribbon microphones. Below UNI-DIRECTIONAL or CARDIOID microphone. The microphone is predominately sensitive to sounds coming from one direction. As a safe rule it is safe to say that the sensitivity of the microphone will have fallen by about 6dB at 90° to its most sensitive axis, and by about 18dB at 180°.

microphone and the tape recorder. Electronic equipment impedances are divided into three rough groups, low, medium and high impedance. Professional equipment uses low impedances wherever possible. There are two reasons: the length of the microphone cable does not matter (within limits, of course) 200 feet (61m) having virtually no effect on the microphone signal; and the effects of interference from other electrical devices is minimised. The impedance used is either 50 ohms or 200 ohms, the latter becoming a standard. One can usually find the impedance marked on the microphone and it will be noted in the tape recorder's handbook. It is as well to be sure, since there is a change in the frequency response of the equipment if there is a mis-match between the impedance of the mike and the tape recorder.

(5) *Directional qualities.* The directional qualities of a microphone can be determined by electrical or physical methods. They are best described graphically on circular graph paper to produce what is called a *polar diagram,*

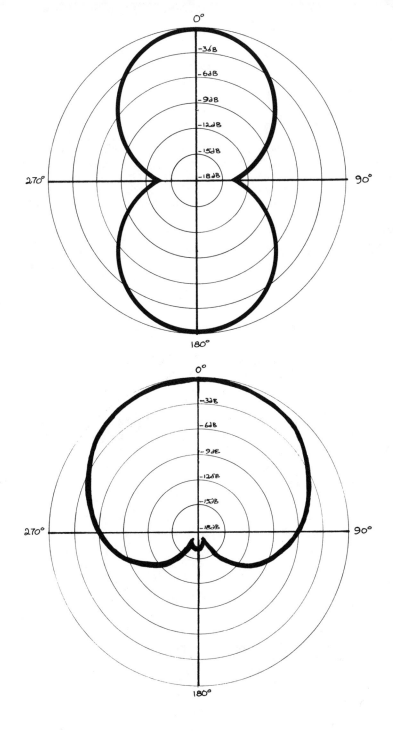

a graph of the sensitivity of a microphone according to the direction from which the sound is coming. There are three main types of directional qualities for microphones, omni-directional, bi-directional (figure of eight) and uni-directional (cardioid). The graphs on the two preceding pages show these three main types, but it must be remembered that they are two-dimensional, whereas the sensitivity is in reality three-dimensional.

If an omni-directional mike is coupled together with a bi-directional microphone a uni-directional polar pattern can be derived. This is because of the construction of the bi-directional microphone in which the sound sensitive element is exposed from and sensitive to sound from two sides only. If the two transducers are together in the same electrical circuit, and assuming that both are close together, then the sound coming from all directions makes the omni-directional mike respond equally. The sound sensitive element of the bi-directional microphone will produce a signal for sounds coming from one side which will be added to that of the omnidirectional transducer, and from the other side which will be subtracted; hence, a directional microphone. The resultant polar diagram is frequently called cardioid because of its resemblance to a heart.

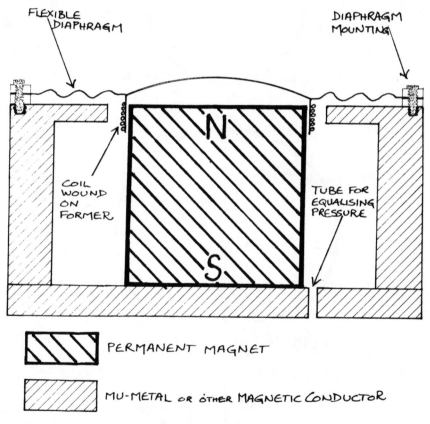

Cross-section of a moving coil microphone.

There are three types of microphone in common use in the professional sound recording industry. These are:

(1) The *moving coil* microphone
(2) The *ribbon* microphone.
(3) The *condenser* microphone.

There are two other types, the carbon microphone and the crystal microphone. The quality of the results from these microphones is not good enough for our consideration (although the carbon microphone is the commonest in everyday use—in the telephone).

All microphones have in common a movable member known either as a diaphragm or ribbon. This lightweight flexible device responds to the changes in atmospheric pressure around itself, rather like a super-sensitive barometer. The diaphragm works on pressure changes on one side, the other side is also in contact with air, but it is air which is trapped inside a chamber with only limited access to the atmosphere. The diaphragms on the moving-coil and condenser microphones are therefore pressure activated. In the ribbon microphone the ribbon is open to pressure changes on both sides, in fact its principle of operation depends on the speed of sound and the dimensions of the ribbon.

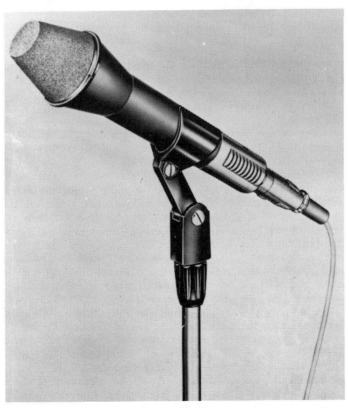

AKG D202 moving coil microphone.

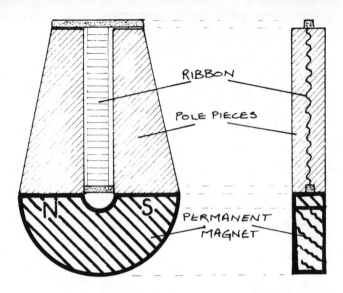

Cross-section of a ribbon microphone.

The fact is that when a wave front hits the ribbon with rapidly-rising pressure there is a difference in pressure between one side of the ribbon and the other, and therefore the ribbon moves. For this reason ribbon mikes are called pressure gradient or velocity mikes.

Both the moving-coil and ribbon mikes work on the same electrical principle of induction. When a conductor is moved in a magnetic field, an electric current is generated in the conductor, the direction of the current depends on the direction in which the conductor is moving. Thus, if the diaphragm is moving inwards because of increasing atmospheric pressure, there will be a current induced in the wire in a particular direction. When the atmospheric pressure changes and the diaphragm starts to move out again, the coil will be moving in the opposite direction in the magnetic field and the current in the coil will also move in the opposite direction. When there are no changes in the atmospheric pressure near the diaphragm, in other words no sound, there will be no movement of the diaphragm and therefore no flow of current.

The condenser (or capacitor or electrostatic) microphone uses the variation in electrostatic charge in a condenser of special construction for sensing variations in atmospheric pressure. When two metal plates connected to an electrical power source are brought close together an electrical charge builds up on the plates. This means that one plate has more electrons than the other. This is in preparation to completing the circuit when the electrons can flow. If the voltage is high enough to break down the insulation between the plates (possibly air), there will be a spark between the plates as the current flows. The useful fact about an electrostatic charge in this circumstance is that the closer together the plates are the higher is the charge, and the further apart they are the lower. If one plate of the condenser is constructed as a rigid plate, and the other as a flexible diaphragm, then the sound waves will change

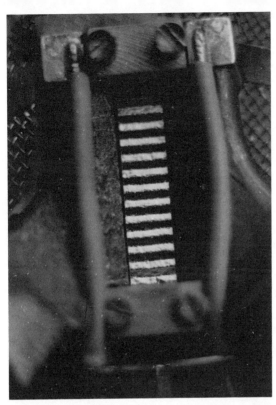

Close-up of the ribbon in a 4038 Broadcast/ Studio Ribbon Microphone. Photo: Hampstead High Fidelity Ltd.

Sennheiser MKH 415 capacitor microphone.

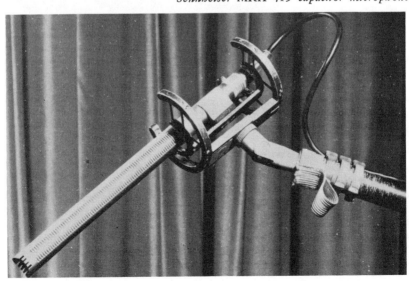

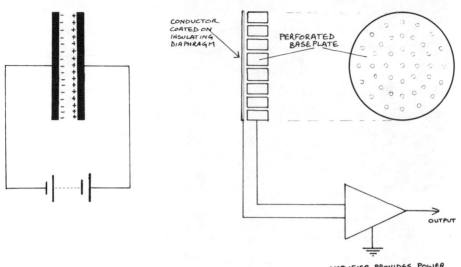

CONDUCTOR COATED ON INSULATING DIAPHRAGM

PERFORATED BASE PLATE

OUTPUT

AMPLIFIER PROVIDES POWER FOR CAPACITOR AND MEASURES VARIATIONS IN ELECTROSTATIC CHARGE.

Capacitor microphone: A *is a circuit with a capacitor and a battery. There is no flow of current across the capacitor, but an electrostatic charge has built up. This will be varied in proportion to the distance of the plates from each other assuming that the battery voltage stays constant.* B: *The basic construction of a capacitor microphone.*

the distance between the plates, varying the electrostatic charge on them. Thus, although there is no flow of current between the plates (hence electro-*static*) there must be a flow of current between the power source and the plates in order for the electrostatic charge to vary. If this can be measured, which with a sensitive amplifier it can, then the result is a microphone.

Another type is the RF condenser microphone (RF standing for radio frequency). In this microphone the condenser, one side of which forms the diaphragm, is part of an RF oscillator circuit. In such a circuit a variation in the capacity of the condenser will bring about a variation in the frequency of the output. In this way a microphone is constructed in which variations in atmospheric pressure are translated into variations in frequency (frequency modulation). A comparatively simple transistor circuit is used to demodulate the signal and produce an audio signal. The advantage of this system is high reliability combined with small size.

It must be realised that a microphone is a very delicate piece of micro-engineering; extremely small components have to be able to move rapidly along a defined path. The diaphragm has to follow the changes in atmospheric pressure which constitute sound (accurately). The diaphragm has to be tough enough to stand the conditions of use and yet flexible enough to enable the very low power of sound waves to move it. The rules given at the beginning of this chapter must be observed.

Although ribbon mikes are bi-directional it is possible by closing one side and preventing sound from getting to that side of the ribbon to make the mike uni-directional. Cardioid ribbon mikes have been made in the past and used extensively. At the present time it is more usual to use condenser or moving-coil transducers for uni-directional mikes. This it not done in combination with a ribbon mike but, by the use of a device called an *acoustic labyrinth.* The diaphragm of a mike in combination with the field magnet or the plate which forms the other side of the condenser could form an air-tight container. This is obviously impractical since there needs to be a way of equalising the atmospheric pressure between the inside and the outside of the mike, rather like the eustacean tube between the middle ear and the nose. The opening at the back of the mike can be designed in such a way that sounds arriving from behind the mike are fed to the back of the diaphragm at the same time as they arrive at the front of the mike. At a moment of increasing pressure this would mean that the diaphragm would experience increasing pressure on both sides at the same time, and the diaphragm would therefore not move. This makes the microphone insensitive to sounds from the rear. A pattern very similar to the cardioid polar pattern is created although there are variations in directional sensitivity according to frequency.

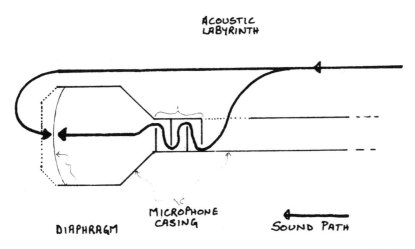

ACOUSTIC LABYRINTH

DIAPHRAGM   **MICROPHONE CASING**   **SOUND PATH**

The ACOUSTIC LABYRINTH makes the length of the paths along which the sound travels from behind the microphone equal to both sides of the diaphragm. Therefore, the diaphragm experiences equal pressure on both sides, and does not move, thus making the microphone insensitive to sounds from behind.

39

Some microphones are fitted with a switch which reduces the bass frequency response, the action of which may be progressive. This control is fitted to improve intelligibility of speech in difficult recording circumstances and to reduce rumble picked up by the microphone. Microphones used close to the source of sound, especially when the source is small in dimension as in speech, become more sensitive to low frequencies and it is only by removing the bass end of the sensitivity that something approaching the normal sound can be reproduced. The handling noises which a microphone is subjected to when on the end of a boom can sometimes lead to large, virtually inaudible bass sounds which will drive a microphone pre-amplifier to distortion. Again the bass cut has to be used to remove these. The same applies when a microphone is used in a wind. The large movements of air move the diaphragm in and out at low frequency causing 'thumps' on the output of the mike.

In some microphones the effect of the bass cut control is severe and listening tests should be made before use. Confusion arises because on some mikes the control is marked M and S (M-music; S-speech). It should really read "Speech when mike is used at less than 1 foot"; with the mike any further away the result is sometimes so lacking in bass as to be virtually unusable.

The effect of boost of bass frequencies when a mike is used close to a voice (known as the *proximity effect*) is reduced by making the diaphragm as small as possible, and indeed in modern microphone design this is happening and the need for bass cut controls is disappearing. The trouble is that when you reduce the size of the diaphragm you have less area available for sensing sound waves and the sensitivity is reduced. Modern portable tape recorders have a bass cut control which can be used, and, in the studio, tone controls are usually available.

The low frequency end of the microphone's output should therefore be removed in three cases: when the mike is used close to a speaker, when thumps from handling can be heard, and in wind.

This summarises the basic principles of the operation of the microphone. Other types of microphone will be described later in this chapter. The next aspect of the sound recordist's kit to be examined is the connection between the microphone and the tape recorder. In this examination it must be realised that a tape recorder has been chosen because it is the basic piece of equipment used for original sound recordings in film. The signal from the microphone is fed first of all into a collection of electronic components called a pre-amplifier. Other equipment which may have a microphone plugged into it, such as a mixing console or a radio transmitter, will also have a pre-amplifier for the microphone. A pre-amplifier simply amplifies (increases the strength of) the signal so that it can be easily handled and manipulated.

I always feel that one of the weakest links in the equipment used for recording sound is the connection between the mike and the tape recorder, and that consequently considerable care must be taken to ensure that it will not break down. The voltage of the signal coming from the microphone is very low, sometimes in the order of micro-volts (millionths of a volt or $N \times 10^{-6}$ volts) and it is necessary to protect the signal from external interference from the electrical environment in which we live. The current that we use to work our electric lamps, refrigerators, washing machines, etc. is alternating current; the voltage is high, varying between 100 and

250 volts depending on the country. In comparison with the voltage of the signal which we are trying to get from the microphone to the tape recorder the mains voltage is enormous.

Surrounding every pair of wires carrying mains current in the building, under the street and between power pylons is a magnetic field which has quite a lot of energy, and moreover at a low frequency which we call hum. The point of all this is that the magnetic field from power cables is enough to interfere with the microphone's very small output, and since the signal from the microphone has to be amplified considerably before it can be used, it is necessary to shield the microphone and the cable from such interference in order to avoid picking up hum. Also, when heavy electrical equipment is switched on or off there is a heavy surge of current along the power cables which radiates energy which can be picked up in the form of clicks. The solution lies in surrounding the sound equipment in a *shield*. The microphone is encased in a magnetic conductor which prevents extraneous

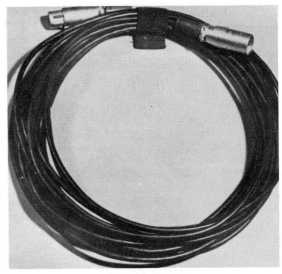

Left: *The braided shielding that surrounds the audio conductors in a microphone cable.* Right: *Microphone cables should be coiled neatly to avoid kinks.*

magnetism from reaching the transducer; the cable from the microphone to the amplifier is twisted and then wrapped in a braiding of wires (the twisted conductors never lie at right angles to the magnetic field for any significant length, and the braided shield surrounding them is a further protection against interference); indeed the whole tape recorder, or certainly those parts dealing with the audio signal, is encased in metal to prevent interference. All these separate shieldings are connected together, and collectively known as *shield, common, ground, earth, chassis,* etc. It is important when purchasing microphone cable to be absolutely certain of getting the best quality shielded cable. There are two types; one, already mentioned, has

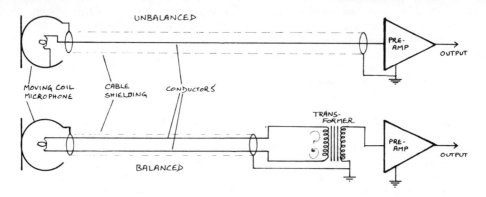

The two basic ways to connect a microphone to an amplifier; known as BAL-ANCED and UNBALANCED lines.

a shielding made out of tiny wires braided around the twisted conductors. In the second type, the shielding consists of a layer of thin wires lapped around the conductors, sometimes there is a second layer laid over the first in the opposite direction. If the microphone cable of the lapped kind has two layers it is unlikely that there will be any problems, but be very suspicious of cable which has only one layer. I remember an occasion while recording in an old town hall when I was plagued by constant intermittent clicks, which accompanied the signals from the microphones. I checked every possible cause finally getting round to the microphone cables. These I discovered had a lapped shielding consisting of one layer. I replaced these with new microphone cable with braided shielding and my problems were over.

The shielding is important for getting rid of interference, and to do this it surrounds the conductors which are carrying the signal. There are two ways of sending the signal to the tape recorder down the conductor, depending upon whether the signal is separated from the shielding or not. The signal can be sent down two separate insulated conductors which run inside the shielding, or can be sent down one conductor, the other half of the circuit being shared with shielding. The first system, known as *balanced line,* is superior if more expensive. (When the signal circuit is shared with the shielding the system is known as *unbalanced line.*) Balanced line will work best into a properly designed balanced input using a transformer (see diagram). Any currents which are generated in the signal conductors by spurious magnetic fields (assuming these are strong enough to break through the shielding) run through the transformer in opposite directions—out of phase—and cancel each other out. The microphone signal on the other hand does not get this treatment and can be amplified interference free.

The microphone will be connected to the cable and then to the tape recorder by plugs which are soldered to the conductors in the cable. It is well to be sure that the solder joins are good and that the cable is well clamped into the plug, thus avoiding movement which could lead to breakages. Since there are more wires in the shielding it is an idea to make use of the

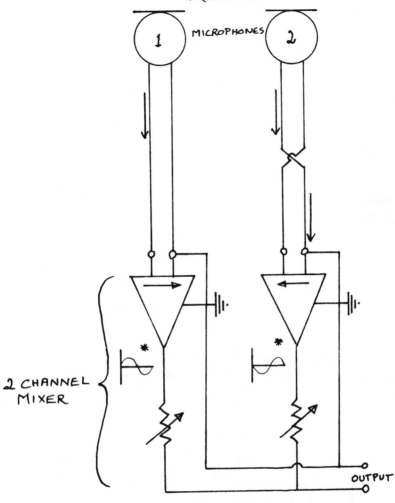

INCREASING ATMOSPHERIC
PRESSURE

MICROPHONES

1

2

2 CHANNEL
MIXER

*

*

OUTPUT

⟶ = DIRECTION OF FLOW OF
CURRENT FROM MICROPHONES
FOR INCREASING ATMOSPHERIC
PRESSURE.

Microphone phasing: these two microphones have been connected out of phase. The graphs (*) show that the signals from the two microphones, when combined in the mixer, will cancel each other out.

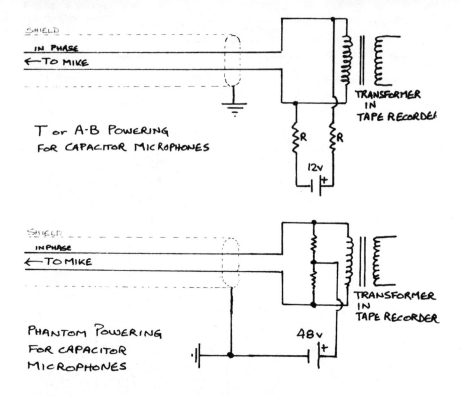

SHIELD

IN PHASE

←TO MIKE

T or A-B POWERING
FOR CAPACITOR MICROPHONES

TRANSFORMER
IN
TAPE RECORDER

R   R

12v

SHIELD

IN PHASE

←TO MIKE

PHANTOM POWERING
FOR CAPACITOR
MICROPHONES

TRANSFORMER
IN
TAPE RECORDER

48v

extra strength and make the connection of the shielding to the pin in the plug rather shorter than that of the conductors. It is important to see that all the plugs are correctly connected and that all the cables are 'in phase'. When using more than one mike, either to enable sounds from widely-separated sources to be recorded simultaneously, or as a protection against failure in live broadcasts, the microphones must be connected so that they supplement each other and do not cancel each other out. The point is that when, for example, the diaphragm is being subjected to increasing pressure and is moving in towards the body of the microphone, the current must move in the same direction through the circuit as it does in another micro-phone in the same circumstances. Manufacturers keep a rigid check on microphones leaving the factory to ensure that all are the same. These checks become pointless if the user gets the cables wired incorrectly. The illustration shows the common microphone plugs and the standard connections. One pin of the plug becomes positive in respect of the other when the diaphragm of the mike is moving inwards (being subjected to increasing atmospheric pressure), and is known as the 'in phase' pin. On the whole this is a universal standard. For balanced microphones there are three pins, one for earth (shielding), one for the 'in phase' signal and one for the neutral signal which together make up the circuit from the mike. In the cable it is

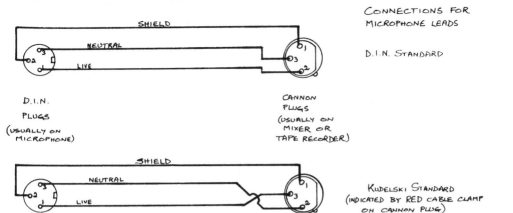

D.I.N. STANDARD

D.I.N.

PLUGS

(USUALLY ON
MICROPHONE)

CANNON
PLUGS
(USUALLY ON
MIXER OR
TAPE RECORDER)

KUDELSKI STANDARD
(INDICATED BY RED CABLE CLAMP
ON CANNON PLUG)

usual to use the red or most colourful conductor for the 'in phase' signal and the dullest which is usually black for the neutral.

Since the microphone cable is such a vital link the cables should be looked after properly; ideally they should be coiled in the same way that a sailor or cowboy coils his rope. This allows for easy uncoiling and prevents an unnecessary strain on the shielding. There can hardly be anything more irritating than trying to uncoil a tangled microphone cable in a hurry in the field.

An AKB11 power supply for Sennheiser capacitor microphones. The switch shown switches on the power supply as well as selecting two degrees of bass cut.

There is one last thing to say about microphone cables; with condenser microphones it is necessary to have a power supply to provide power for the amplifier and plates inside the microphone. Most condenser mikes are transistorised and the power needed varies from 1.5 volts to 11 volts. Various types of supply are available. They all have one thing in common and that is that they supply the current for the microphone along the same cable as the audio, a system known as phantom powering; the diagram will help in the understanding of this. The power pack separates the direct current used for power and the audio, thus feeding only the audio signal to the tape recorder preamplifier. There are some portable tape recorders now designed which are fitted with pre-amplifiers designed for condenser mikes, and which supply the current needed for the mike from the recorder's battery supply. Microphone cables must be correctly connected when condenser mikes are being used in order to ensure that the correct current polarity is being fed to the microphone. If the polarity of the current is incorrect the microphone will not work.

When using external power packs the voltage of the batteries should be checked from time to time, and indeed some are fitted with special terminals to enable this to be done. The other indication that the battery strength is failing is that the signal from the microphone becomes very noisy (there is a lot of hiss).

Modern portable tape recorders have a bass cut filter which can be switched in and out at will. Some condenser microphone power packs are fitted with bass cut to cope with those recorders which have none. The bass cut will only operate satisfactorily with mike pre-amps which have a transformer input. This bass cut is very useful since the bass response of the condenser microphone is so good that there is a good chance of bass distortion from handling and wind noise. The batteries should last for some 24 hours of continuous use.

The Tape Recorder

A moment's thought will bring the realisation that sound cannot be stopped in the same way that an instantaneous photograph will stop an action. All systems for recording sound so far invented have a medium for storing the sound information which moves both during the recording and replay processes. The tape recorder falls into this category. Most sound recorded for films is mastered onto tape. The equipment used is usually portable and of a very high standard of manufacture. Sound recorded for films in recording studios may be recorded on mains-operated studio recorders, but the layout and the terminology remains much the same as that for portables. In the following pages, it will be assumed that a portable tape recorder is one powered by batteries and therefore completely self-contained, and that a studio tape recorder is mains-powered and a fixture.

To store sound waves, or the electrical analogy of sound waves, the signal from the microphone, the tape recorder uses magnetism. The tape, which is a thin flexible strip of plastics (usually polyester) is coated with an emulsion of iron oxide (or chromium dioxide). These iron oxide particles will, when exposed to strong magnetic fields, retain the magnetism. In simple terms, to record a sound it is necessary to convert the sound waves into magnetism which can be imposed on the emulsion of the tape. The signal from the

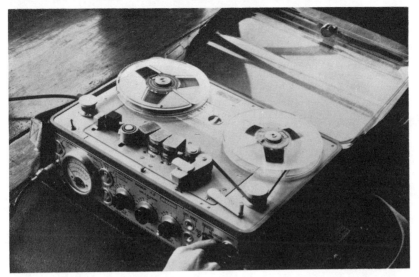

Above: *The Nagra 4.2 tape recorder. This is the workhorse of the film industry. It is battery-powered and very portable.* Below: *A Leevers-Rich mains operated studio tape recorder. This type of recorder is designed for use in the studio and is essentially a fixture.*

Close-up of heads on a Nagra 4.2. A: Erase head. B: Record head. C: Pilot Tone head (see page 102). D: Playback head.

microphone is first amplified and then applied to the tape by a specialised electro-magnet called a *head*. On a professional tape recorder a minimum of three heads will be found. Since the tape moves from left to right in most recorders they will be arranged as follows:

(left)	*erase head*	To clean the tape prior to recording.
(centre)	*record head*	To impose a pattern of magnetism on the tape which is a copy of the sound waves.
(right)	*replay* or *playback head*	To reproduce the recording that has been made.

Other heads are added to this array for synchronous sound recording and are dealt with in a later chapter.

The mechanism which moves the tape has to be well designed and accurately made. This mechanism is called the *tape transport* and is mounted on a plate called the *deck*. The main function of the transport is to move the tape at a very constant and defined speed past the heads. The secondary function is fast forward winding and rewinding of the tape.

Tape recorders are available in two groups: *open reel* and *cassette*. Professionals usually use open reel recorders although there are many uses to which cassette recorders can be put and with good results. The tape is supplied on a reel which is mounted on the feed spindle of the recorder (see diagram). This spindle is attached to a driving mechanism which will apply power to rewind the tape, or a small amount of braking force for tensioning

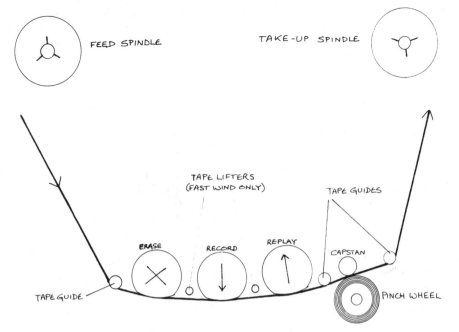

The components of a tape deck.

the tape when recording or replaying. Studio tape recorders which are equipped to spool the tape at high speed in the forward direction will have a brake which is applied to the feed spindle when fast winding is over to prevent the tape from spilling off the reel. The empty reel for taking up the used tape is placed on the take-up spindle which is driven either by a motor or a clutch mechanism which applies constant tension to the tape. Provision will be made on studio tape recorders, but not necessarily on portable recorders for fast forward winding. Both the feed tension and the take-up tension is sometimes controlled by the tension in the tape itself sensed by spring-loaded rollers. These rollers adjust the torque being applied to the feed and take-up spindles.

The vertical position of the tape relative to the heads is controlled by guide posts, sometimes part of the mechanism which holds the tape away from the heads during fast winding. This saves the heads from excessive exposure to friction.

The tape is moved at constant speed past the heads by the *capstan*. This is an accurately machined shaft which is rotated by a motor. The tape is held in contact with the capstan by a rubber roller called a *pinch wheel* or *puck*.

In the design of the capstan and its drive mechanism great care has to be taken to ensure that the shaft is straight and true, and that it rotates at a very constant speed. In a studio tape recorder where weight does not matter it is possible to use a heavy flywheel, or a Pabst motor, which has a heavy external rotor, to achieve smooth running. In portable recorders designers have had to develop small but powerful electric motors with elec-

49

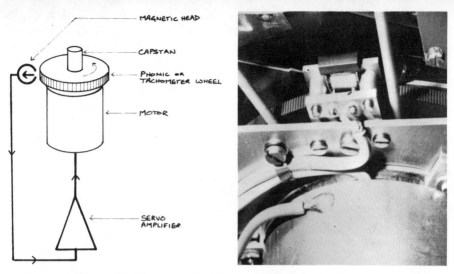

Motor of Nagra 4.2. The serrated tachometer wheel passes close to a magnetic head which reads the serrations as tone. The frequency of the tone is determined by the servo amplifier, which adjusts the voltage fed to the motor to maintain the correct speed. The process is continuous.

tronic speed governors to do the same job. As it happens they work very well and give a performance equal to that of the heavy mechanism in studio recorders.

The interaction between the capstan motor drive and the feed and take-up tensions is vital to the constant speed running of the tape. Portable recorders usually use one motor to perform all functions (using rubber belts and clutches), but studio recorders use separate motors for feed and take-up and therefore have a great deal of power available for fast spooling. Subtle control can be obtained for feed and take-up.

It is not possible to make a tape recorder which will run at an absolutely constant speed. Speed variations can be reduced, however, to a very low level, and should be inaudible. There are two types of speed variation: long term and short term; long term variations take place over the whole length of the reel of tape and are caused by the varying amount of tape on the feed and take-up reels and tape slip at the capstan. The speed variation caused this way should be as small as possible—not more than 0.5%. Short term variations, unlike the long term variations, can be audible. They divide into two categories: wow and flutter; *wow* = speed variations which repeat themselves less than ten times per second, *flutter* = speed variations faster than ten times per second. In a good tape recorder the combined wow and flutter figure should not exceed 0.1%. This is the percentage deviation from the mean speed of the recorder. In a portable recorder the wow and flutter should remain substantially constant regardless of the attitude of the recorder and within limits regardless of the amount of movement the recorder is being subjected to.

For the best results a tape recorder must be threaded correctly. The tape path is either very simple, marked on the deck, or available from the instruction book. The common portable tape recorder threading paths are illustrated in the appendix of this book.

Tape Recorder Controls

Control of the various functions may vary from machine to machine. There is quite a difference between studio and portable tape recorders because of the need to preserve battery strength and keep weight low in the portables. Main control of a tape deck and the associated amplifiers can be divided into five sections:

STOP: Stops the tape. In a portable this function will switch off the power too. There may be a safety lock which forces the operator to use this control when switching from a fast winding function to record or replay. This prevents accidental overspill of the tape.

PLAY: Engages the pinch wheel with the capstan, removes any braking applied to the tape and switches on spindle motors to apply the correct tension to the tape for running. Connects the replay amplifier.

RECORD: The same as PLAY but also switches on the erase and record heads. A safety lock prevents the operator from accidentally engaging the record mode e.g. it may be necessary to press both the PLAY and RECORD buttons at the same time. In the case of Nagra portable tape recorders, the switch which selects record and replay has to be moved in opposite directions around the stop position in order to make the selection. In addition, between STOP and RECORD there is a position called TEST (enabling the operator to monitor signals arriving at the recorder without recording) which acts as a safety factor to prevent accidental erasure of previously recorded tape (see illustration on page 52).

FAST FORWARD⎤ Disconnects the pinch wheel and brakes, lifts the tape
FAST REWIND ⎦ away from the heads and switches the appropriate motor to full power.

In portable machines some of these functions will need man-power, but in most studio machines, apart from selection of a switch, the action is electrical.

The reaction between the magnetic head and the tape emulsion during recording

Research has shown the reaction between the head and the magnetic emulsion of the tape to be complicated. It can be simplified as follows.

The ability of materials to conduct magnetism is broken up into three main groups. *Permeability* is the name given to magnetic conductibility.

Ferromagnetic Good permeability
Paramagnetic Medium permeability
Diamagnetic Bad permeability.

The magnetic head is made from a ferromagnetic material like soft iron or ferrite. It is made in two halves, as can be seen from the diagram. Around each half is wrapped a field coil. When an electric current flows through the coils a magnetic field is created which is easily guided since the pole pieces are

The controls on a Revox tape recorder. The buttons are (from left to right) FAST REWIND, FAST FORWARD, PLAYBACK, STOP, RECORD. It is necessary to press both the playback and record buttons simultaneously in order to record.

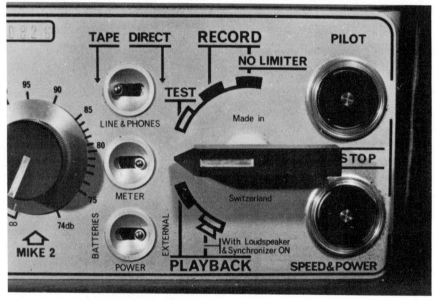

Main Function Switch of Nagra 4.2.

made of ferromagnetic material. If the two halves were just pressed together there would be a complete magnetic circuit. However there is a diamagnetic material such as brass, mica or gold inserted into the gap between the two halves. This has the effect of forcing the magnetic lines of force outside the geometry of the pole pieces. When tape is pressed in contact with the gap,

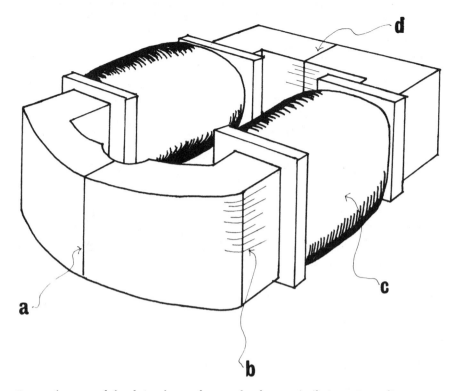

Parts of a record head (replay and erase heads are similar): a *Recording gap.* b *Polepieces (showing laminations).* c *Field coil.* d *Gap. Drawing: Sue Chambers.*

the iron oxide in the emulsion, a paramagnetic substance, forms a comparatively good magnetic conductor and completes the magnetic circuit. Therefore in a sense the diamagnetic gap filler is the most important aspect of the head since it forces the magnetism into the storage medium. The iron oxide particles take on magnetism as they leave the gap in the head.

The replay head is similar in construction. Tape passing the gap presents the head with a series of fluctuating magnetic fields which induce small currents in the coils surrounding the pole pieces. These are amplified to produce the sound. The main difference in the replay head is that the gap has to be much smaller than that in the record head. This is to enable the replay head to scan the changing waveform of the shortest wavelengths (and therefore the highest frequencies).

Unfortunately, in the recording process, the reaction of the magnetic iron oxide particles in the emulsion of the tape to the applied magnetism is not proportional or linear. At low levels of applied magnetism there is hardly any reaction; there is an inertia that has to be overcome. Once it *has* been overcome the reaction becomes more or less linear until the emulsion becomes saturated with magnetism; in other words, cannot be further magnetised. To apply the audio signal alone to the record head is not enough since, because of the non-linearity, the sound wave is stored in a very distorted way. This cannot be corrected in replay, and the solution lies in activating the tape during the recording process with a very high frequency current which is applied to the record head at the same time as the audio signal. The current is called *bias* and is, at the present time, universal to high quality audio recording.

The strength of the application of bias to the record head is a compromise. (See Table) Experiments have established optimum settings for bias and a sort of standard has been set. Some equipment is set up for one type of tape and it is quite complicated to change the bias setting. This applies especially to portable tape recorders. Studio tape recorders and film recorders are relatively simple to adjust and once adjusted for a particular batch of tape or film are stable. The equipment needed for the adjustment of bias is as follows:

An audio oscillator.

A meter to read decibel level from the output of the recorder.

A sample of the tape or film on which the recording will be made.

Some recorders have the oscillator and the meter built in. To understand the procedure the result of the addition of bias in varying strengths should be studied. The graph shows the replay strength of a recorded signal versus bias strength and the region of optimum bias setting is marked.

The procedure for setting bias is as follows:

(1) Turn the bias control to provide minimum bias strength.
      On some recorders there will be a meter which shows the strength of bias. (There are cases where the bias control turns anticlockwise to increase bias strength and it may be necessary to establish this first.)
(2) Load the tape into the recorder.
(3) Plug the oscillator into the input of the recorder.
(4) Set the frequency of the oscillator to 1KHz.
(5) Increase the gain of the recorder so that the input meter reads 100%.
(6) Switch the meter to read output or plug the previously mentioned decibel meter to the output of the recorder.
(7) Start the recorder and switch to record.
(8) While watching the replay meter, increase the strength of the bias.
(9) The meter will register increasing replay strength as the bias is increased. When the replay strength has reached its peak it will start to drop away. The best setting for bias will usually be just beyond the point at which replay started to drop, usually 1dB at 7.5ips (19.05cm/s) and 2dB at 15ips (38.1 cm/s). The amount depends on the speed of the tape or film, the frequency of the test tone, the type of tape or film, and the recommended best practice for the recorder. For instance with 35mm magnetic film which runs at 18ips (45.72 cm/s) the amount by which the replay signal must fall away is usually taken to be 2dB, and with 16mm, ½dB. If a higher frequency is used (10KHz is often recommended these days), then the correct bias setting for 15ips tape is in the order of 4 or 5dB over the top, 7.5ips, 1½ or 2dB. The amount can only be found out by experience and experiment.

Some mention should be made about problems encountered with tape. Drop out, referred to in the table about bias, is the effect caused by momentary loss of contact between the tape and either the record head or the replay head. This is caused by dirt, or deformation of the plastics base on which the emulsion is bonded. Better stock manufacture, which ensures more uniformity

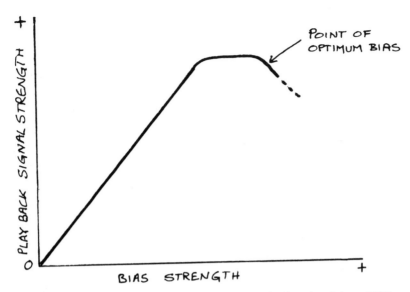

Graph showing the relationship between playback of a signal (e.g. 1KHz tone) and the bias being used while recording the signal.

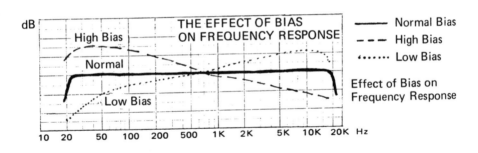

High Bias		Low Bias
Dramatically Reduced	Incidence of Drop-out	Increased
Lower	Noise	Higher
Reduced	Distortion	Increased
Reduced	High Frequency Response	Increased
Increased	Low Frequency Response	Reduced

The effects of differing bias strength.

of the base and less likelihood of the emulsion peeling off, has reduced the chances of drop out considerably. It is nevertheless important to protect the tapes and tape heads from dust and dirt. The best place to keep tape or film when it is not in use is in the box or can. Tape heads should be cleaned regularly with a soft cloth moistened with methylated spirits or alcohol, or with an aerosol spray specially manufactured for the purpose (such as Colclene TF).

There is sometimes a reaction between the plastics base of the tape and the parts of the recorder with which it comes into contact, especially if the recorder uses felt pads to keep the tape in contact with the heads, which creates an electrostatic build-up. When the potential discharges, the amplifiers produce a click. There is little one can do to cure this problem except change the pads or use different tape. The best results lie in trial and error.

The magnetic heads on a tape or film recorder will eventually wear out. Test procedures to be outlined in the next section will show up the effects of wear and will give the operator adequate warning. Once a head has worn out it should be replaced as its actual performance deteriorates. This is because the wear removes enough of the metal from the head to expose the bottom of the gap, which therefore starts to widen, with a consequent loss of high frequency response, an effect more noticeable in the replay than record head. The performance of a recorder should therefore be checked fairly regularly.

Azimuth.

The angle of the gap in the head must be adjusted so that it lies at an angle of 90° to the direction of travel of the tape, this is a standard. If the angle of the record head is different to that of the replay head then the quality of the recording suffers on playback. The high frequencies are lost, since the effective gap in the head has widened. The gap in the replay head must be shorter than the shortest wavelength it is expected to reproduce so that it can scan the information in the waveform and therefore produce a varying voltage from it. The adjustment of azimuth is simple enough. On a recorder which has badly-designed head mounts, it may be necessary to check it frequently. A definite routine should be established for running tests.

In order to establish the correct running of a tape recorder a *test tape* is used. These tapes are expensive. Many types are available but on the whole perform the same function. Because of the expense involved it is well to take precautions that the recorder will do no damage.

(1) Clean the heads of the recorder.
(2) Demagnetise the heads of the recorder using a head degausser. Caution must be used if the heads are truly to be demagnetised and not left in a magnetised state. If at all possible, remove the heads from the recorder beforehand, since the current produced from the heads in the powerful magnetic field of the degausser can damage the first transistor in the pre-amps. Switch the recorder off. Switch the degausser on. A most important aspect of using one of these devices is that it is not switched off again until the demagnetisation process is over and the degausser is well away from the recorder. Move the tip of the degausser slowly to the head, leave it there a moment and then slowly move onto the next head, and repeat the performance until every head and component on the recorder that could be magnetised and touches the tape has been

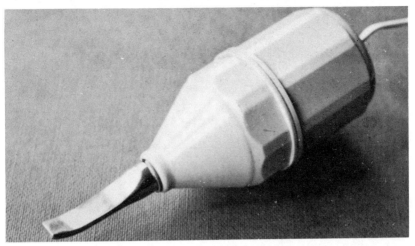

A tape head degausser. Care must be taken to use this device properly.

covered. Then move the degausser away from the recorder slowly until it is about 5 feet (1.5m) away. Then and only then switch off the degausser. At all times move the degausser slowly, and make sure that it is well away from the recorder before switching off.

Note: There are two points; in the case of the Nagra tape recorders, which use an electronic speed governor on the drive motor, there is a magnetic head (tachometer head) which is used, in conjunction with a phonic wheel, to sense the speed at which the motor is running. In order to function correctly this head should be partially magnetised. Great care should therefore be taken not to subject the recorder to a very strong de-magnetising magnetic field.

The second point is that if a tape recorder is operating well and there is no reason to suspect magnetised heads, it is probably best left alone.

Other pieces of equipment needed for the adjustment of azimuth and testing the recorder are an audio oscillator (as used for setting bias and a meter (preferably a transistorised AC meter), and a roll of blank tape or film.

The test tape will have a number of different tests recorded on it:
(1) 1KHz tone recorded 320 pWb/mm or OdBVU (—4 ref 320pWb/m) in order to check the replay level of the recorder.
(2) 10KHz or 15KHz tone recorded at —10dBm to check the azimuth.
(3) A series of tones of different frequency recorded at —14dBm for checking the frequency response of the replay head and amplifier.

Place the test tape on the recorder and run the recorder in replay. (This is important because of the expense of the tape). Plug the meter into the replay output of the recorder.
(1) Refer to the instruction manual for the recorder and ascertain the correct output voltage from the replay amplifier for 100% modulated tape. With the transistorised AC voltmeter check and adjust the replay level.
(2) Find the azimuth adjustment screw for the replay head and adjust the azimuth so that the meter reads as high as possible for this section of the tape. The replay head is then adjusted to the azimuth standard of the test tape.

CUSTOMER ..CHARLES...B...FRATER...

SERIAL NO..III.N.P.64.5655.H.. ENGINEER .R.L.MUIR....... DATE .3/6/70..

FREQUENCY RESPONSE

REPLAY   15"/Sec. CCIR to DIN.45.573....... RECORD TESTED WITH

7.5"/Sec. CCIR to DIN.45.573....... STD SCOTCH.262...

7.5"/Sec. NAB to .... LN.......................

3.75"/Sec. CCIR to ....

| FREQ | 15"/Sec CCIR | | | 7.5"/Sec CCIR | | | 7.5"/Sec NAB | | 3.75"/Sec CCIR | | |
Hz	REPLAY	STD RECORD	LN RECORD	REPLAY	STD RECORD	LN RECORD	REPLAY	RECORD	REPLAY	STD RECORD	LN RECORD
20		−5·0			−3·5					−5·2	
25		−2·1			−2·9					−2·8	
31.5	−0·4	−0·2		−3·0	−2·6					−2·3	
40	−0·2	+0·2		−1·0	−0·5					−0·7	
63	−1·2	−0·9		−0·1	+0·5					+1·0	
125	0	0		+0·8	+0·8					+0·5	
250	+0·4	+0·5		+0·8	+0·9					+0·2	
500	+0·3	+0·5		+0·4	+0·3					0	
1K	0	0		0	0					0	
2K	−0·2	−0·4		−0·2	−0·3					+0·5	
4K	−0·1	−0·8		−0·4	−0·4					+0·7	
6.3K	−0·2	−0·7		+0·3	−0·2					−2·5	
8K	+0·1	−0·4		+0·3	0					−9·0	
10K	+0·5	+0·3		+0·2	+0·2						
125K	+0·6	+0·8		−0·4	−0·1						
14K	+0·4	+1·0		−0·8	−1·0						
16K	0	+0·8		−2·5	−2·7						
18K	−0·2	0		−4·3	−6·8						
20K		−2·0									
25K											
30K											

DISTORTION %

| | STD | | | LN | | |
	2nd H	3rd H	TOTAL	2nd H	3rd H	TOTAL
15"/Sec CCIR	0·7	1·6	1·9			
7.5"/Sec CCIR	0·25	1·7	2·1			
7.5"/Sec NAB						
3.75"/Sec CCIR	0·20	0·65	1·4			

SIGNAL TO NOISE RATIO dB

| | TAPE RUNNING | TAPE STOPPED |
SPEED		
15"/Sec CCIR	−69·5	−74·5
7.5"/Sec CCIR	−67·5	−71·5
7.5"/Sec NAB		
3.75"/Sec CCIR	−68·0	−70·0

WOW AND FLUTTER %

	WOW	FLUTTER	TOTAL
15"/Sec	0·015	0·03	0·035
7.5"/Sec	0·020	0·07	0·075
3.75"/Sec	0·040	0·09	0·110

R.M.S   UNWEIGHTED

SPEED STABILITY %

	ERROR
15"/Sec	0·09
7.5"/Sec	0·14
3.75"/Sec	0·24

MICROPHONE INPUTS

	SENSITIVITY	−1dB	−1dB
CHANNEL 1	0·124 mV	48 Hz	27 KHz
CHANNEL 2	mV	Hz	KHc

A typical test report sheet.

(3)   Watching the meter, write down the replay levels at each frequency.
There is usually an announcement on the tape before each one. The
types of test tape vary, but the frequencies recorded on them will be
something like this: 20Hz, 25Hz, 31.5Hz, 40Hz, 63Hz, 125Hz,
250Hz, 500Hz, 800Hz, 1KHz, 2KHz, 4KHz, 6.3KHz, 8KHz, 10KHz,
15.5KHz, 14KHz, 16KHz, 18KHz.

There may be adjustment points on the replay amplifier chain for the setting
of a flat replay response. Changes in the replay frequency response will more
than likely be due to wearing in the replay head and when the replay frequency
response from 10KHz upwards starts to drop markedly, the time has come
for replacement. Rewind the test tape and return it to its labelled tin and
put it away safely.

Place the reel of new tape on the recorder. Plug the ocsillator into the
recorder and record a 1KHz tone. Adjust the bias of the recorder in the
previously described way. Switch the oscillator to 10KHz and adjust the

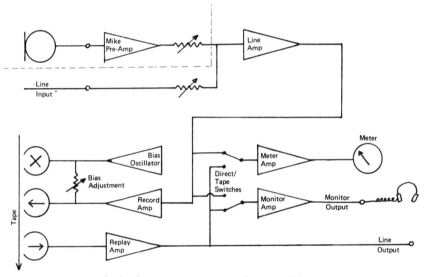

Block diagram—tape recorder amplifiers.

record head azimuth until the replay signal reaches the highest level on the
replay meter. The higher the frequency used for checking azimuth the
better, so it is advisable to reset the oscillator to a higher frequency such as
15KHz and re-run the test. The record head is now adjusted to the same
standard as the replay head. (The assumption must be made that the original test tape used for setting up the replay head was reasonably accurate.)
Now return to 1 KHz and adjust the recording level so that the replay level
is again at 100%, as it was from the test tape. Check that the meter on the
input of the recorder itself reads 100% and adjust if necessary (reference to
the recorder's instruction manual will show the position of the preset volume
controls for this). Record a series of frequencies from the oscillator similar

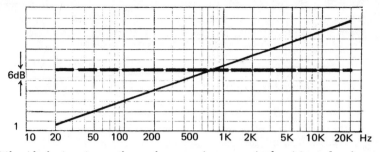

1. *The ideal situation, where the tape is magnetised with a flat frequency response. The laws of magnetism dictate that the replay signal will rise in strength by 6dB per octave.*

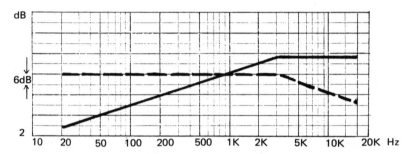

2. *Because of tape deficiencies the resultant magnetism (— — — —) from the record head falls at about 6dB per octave above the turnover frequency. This varies with the tape and its speed but in this case is about 3Hz per octave. A flat amplifier would therefore produce the replay response curve illustrated (— — — —).*

to those on the test tape. Assuming that the oscillator has a flat frequency response the results will produce a record-replay response curve for the recorder.

Further equipment is needed to check the distortion and wow and flutter figures for the recorder and is best left to those who have the facilities. The specifications of modern recorders remain pretty constant but checks should be carried out regularly or whenever there is a suspicion of anything being wrong.

Tape Recorder Amplifier and Meter Circuits:

In sound recording for films we are mostly concerned with the amplifiers of portable tape recorders and studio film recorders. However, professional sound recorders have many points in common. Reference to the diagram will be necessary. Please note that this has been simplified to show the main points.

The recording process cannot take place satisfactorily without bias added to the audio signal and it it therefore necessary to combine the two.

A small tuned circuit called a bias trap prevents the bias from feeding back into the audio amplifier. The variable resistance allows the operator to adjust

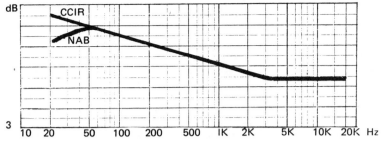

3. It is therefore necessary to modify the frequency response of the replay amplifier in order to get a flat frequency response.

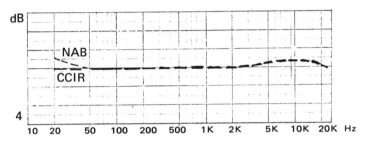

4. The record amplifier frequency response is adjusted to give a small rise at high frequencies to compensate for replay head gap losses.

the strength of the bias being fed into the record head. The bias is generated by an oscillator and is fed in greater strength to the erase head which the tape must pass before reaching the record head. Since the erase current may need to be as much as 3 watts the construction of an erase head is more robust than a record or replay head. There must be as little reaction as possible between the bias signal and the audio. For this reason the frequency of bias is kept as high as possible—traditionally about 60KHz but more recently as high as 120KHz. It is important that the waveform of the bias be as symmetrical and as pure as possible if the signal-to-noise ratio is to be kept high and the distortion low.

In accordance with the physical laws of magnetism and induction, the output signal of the replay head rises 6dB per octave (6dB every time the frequency of the signal on the tape doubles) even though the amplitude or strength of the magnetism remains constant. Therefore it is necessary to design into the replay amplifier an equalisation characteristic which makes the amplifier more sensitive at low frequencies than at high frequencies; a sort of equal and opposite compensation for the 6dB per octave rise in output from the replay head. Unfortunately this effect is only true while the wavelength of the signal on the tape is comparatively large and at frequencies above approximately 1KHz other effects start to play a part. As the wavelength gets smaller the proximity of one magnetic field to the next starts a process of self-demagnetisation which produces a smaller magnetic field in

61

comparison to that of the longer wavelengths. Thus the output from the replay head starts to fall after a certain frequency has been reached (an effect which becomes more severe the slower the tape is moving since the wavelengths for the same given frequency are shorter). Also the size of the gap in the replay head becomes larger in relationship to the wavelength as the frequency rises and there is less ability to track the changing waveform. Consequently there is a need for a further compensation to be applied to the replay amplifier to increase its sensitivity in the upper frequency zone. This is achieved by the addition of a filter network usually described by its time constant factor. The graph shows the type of frequency response curve designed into a magnetic sound replay amplifier in order to overcome the 6dB per octave rise and high frequency head losses in a replay head and the self-demagnetisation in the tape for several different tape speeds. International standards now govern the exact requirements and thus tapes can be exchanged round the world with no trouble. Not only is there equalisation in the replay amplifier, but pre-emphasis is also applied to the record signal, a small amount of high frequency boost being applied to compensate to a degree for the demagnetisation effect.

The recording amplifier is designed to accept signals at a specific strength if 100% recording level is to be achieved. This is usually zero level (0dBm) also expressed as one milliwatt or .775 volts across 600 ohms. The amplifier will increase the strength of the signal to that required by the record head. Driving the record amplifier will be a line amplifier, the function of which is to accept signals from other amplifiers. It will also drive the monitor circuit and the meter.

The meter in a magnetic recorder measures the strength of the audio signal being fed to the record amplifier. Unfortunately the thinking behind such meters and indicators is complex. First of all it must be realised why a meter is needed.

The meter has to give a visual indication of the signal which is going to the record head. It has to indicate when the tape is becoming saturated with magnetism and therefore the point at which distortion is about to begin.

It does not matter what type of meter a recorder has, provided the user realises how it indicates. There are two basic groups: the Volume Unit meter (VU meter) and the Peak Programme Meter (PPM). The difference in these two meters lies in the way in which the needles move. In the VU meter the movement of the needle bears a resemblance to the subjective effect of the volume of a sound on the ear. The meter reads the average strength of the sound signal, which is largely because the needle has mass and does not have time to react fully to a sound level if the sound is short in duration. Only on constant notes such as tone or long musical chords does the needle read anything like the correct value. Because of the intermittent nature of speech the VU meter will read an average of 8dB less than the true peak value of the speech signals. Thus the man operating a recorder with a VU meter will be accustomed to setting his microphone volume control so that the needle of the meter hovers around the —8dB mark when he is recording speech. If the needle of the meter moves to 0dB on the scale there is a possibility that the recording may be distorted since the true reading would be in the region of +8dB. The sensitivity of VU meters is increased by 4dB to compensate for their comparative insensitivity to short duration peaks in sound level. The result

Left: *A V.U. Meter.* Right: *A Peak Program Meter (PPM).*

is that it over-reads for long duration sounds of the type found in music, but still tends to under-read on the short peaks found in speech. It may seem then that the VU meter is limited in its use; it is very common however, and it only takes a little practice before becoming accustomed to it.

The PPM on the other hand is designed to read the peak in the strength of the signals. It is driven by an amplifier which forces the needle up the scale and delays the time it takes for the needle to return, therefore the needle may only be halfway down the scale before the next sound arrives and will be able to read its strength more accurately since it has less distance to travel. The recordist using the PPM will be used to its accuracy when recording both speech and music and will be happy to allow it to indicate 100% recording level, without fear that he may be over-recording.

Never trust a meter on unfamiliar equipment before first running a listening test. The ultimate test of any sound recorder and its meter must be the ear, which will hear distortion easily and give an indication of the operation of the meter.

Other volume indicators are available and tend to use light in some way or other. The magic eye, constructed like a radio valve, was used extensively in domestic tape recorders when they first appeared and displays the sound level as two green illuminated wings which get closer together the louder the sound. Since the illuminated wings are in fact created by a beam of electrons the movement of the meter is weightless and therefore peak reading. Unfortunately these indicators are not calibrated in decibels and are therefore useless to the professional.

Popular in dubbing theatres at one time was a meter which used a row of neon bulbs as the indication. Recently similar designs have appeared using light-emitting diodes instead of neon bulbs.

Some projectors equipped to record magnetic stripe on 16mm have used a pair of neon bulbs to indicate recording level. The volume of the recording is adjusted so that one bulb glows most of the time and the other only occasionally. The second bulb indicates 100% recording level, should it glow all the time the recording will certainly be distorted.

Nothing can quite replace the meter as a volume indicator since a quick glance at it will tell the recordist all he needs to know. In a sense the meter need not even be calibrated since it is the angle of the needle that the recordist looks at rather than the numbers.

The monitor circuit, also driven by the line amp, is a vital part of any good tape recorder. It enables the operator to listen to what he is recording. Since the replay amplifier of the recorder will also produce a zero level signal if the tape has been recorded to a 100% level, it is possible by the addition of a switch, to make a comparison between the signal going to the record head and the signal coming off the replay head. The switch is variously known as a RECORD/RE-PLAY, DIRECT/FILM, DIRECT/TAPE or A/B TEST switch. Some people who trained in the days of optical sound recording still refer to the replay function of this switch as 'pec', which stands for photo-electric cell, a component used in the monitoring circuit of the optical sound camera.

The monitor output of a portable tape recorder will be able to drive a set of headphones. Good quality headphones should be used since the sound obtained from them is the only indication that the operator has of the quality of the recording. If possible they should be the type fitted with large sound-proof ear pads since these provide the operator with greater insulation between the sound being recorded and that which he is hearing. Sometimes the recorder will have a volume control to adjust the volume of the sound coming from the head-phones. This should be set to a comfortable level which is a happy medium between deafening the operator and loud. Monitoring at too soft a level can be dangerous since some irritating background sounds which will appear in the re-play at the studio may be inaudible in the headphones. Too great a volume can lead to listening fatigue and is not good for the ear. Once the right compromise level has been set the operator should never alter it. This is important because the ear becomes accustomed to the volume and, with familiarity, reference to the meter becomes less necessary.

There is an aspect of the monitor output which always causes amusement. In the TAPE or B TEST position there is a delay between the sound that is being recorded and the signal heard in the headphones. This is caused by the spacing between the record and replay heads and the need for the tape to travel from one to the other. The delay makes it almost impossible for the operator to talk while recording since he hears his own voice a fraction of a second after he has spoken. The primary purpose of the A/B TEST switch is to enable the operator to check that there is little quality difference between the original signal and the recorded signal, but it has the secondary purpose of enabling him to make announcements on the tape without sounding like an idiot.

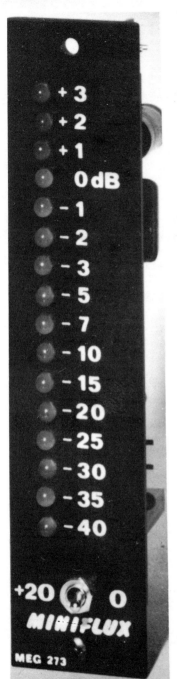

Left. *A peak reading meter using light emitting diodes.*
Above: *Tape/Direct Switch in Nagra IS.*

Photo: Miniflux.

Headphones plugged into a Nagra 4.2. Note that the headphones have substantial ear pads which both exclude extraneous noise and make them more comfortable to wear. I personally prefer a curly cable, since it keeps itself out of the way.

Other Amplifiers

The microphone pre-amplifier has to amplify the extremely small voltage from the microphone and feed it to the line amplifier, via a volume control, at the appropriate signal strength. There has to be a compromise in its sensitivity. If it is sensitive enough to pick up the quietest whisper it becomes too sensitive for the roar of a jet aeroplane. Such an amplifier would be too sensitive for use with a capacitor microphone (which usually has a higher output than a moving coil microphone for the same given sound level), since the higher output could drive the pre-amplifier to distortion. The microphone pre-amplifier is therefore designed to provide adequate sensitivity for recording dialogue with moving coil and capacitor microphones. It will have extra sensitivity in hand for softer sounds and will be able to handle high signal levels too. It may be necessary to add an extra device called an attenuator to the input to reduce the sensitivity of the pre-amp in noisy conditions or with condenser microphones. A word of warning here however; some microphone pre-amplifiers are designed to provide the phantom power for the condenser microphone, thus the interposing of an attenuator will reduce the voltage to the microphone and it will cease to function correctly. There are some condenser microphone power supplies fitted with a bass cut, but these rely on the primary winding of the microphone pre-amplifier input transformer to provide part of the bass cut circuit, and consequently interposing an attenuator will also have an effect on the circuit. Therefore, in

Two microphone pre-amplifiers inside a Nagra 4.2. The left hand one is for a capacitor microphone. It supplies the power for the microphone and also has a bass cut switch. The right hand amplifier is for moving coil and ribbon microphones, or capacitor microphones which have an external power supply.

areas of high ambient sound, use a moving coil microphone which is less sensitive and with which it is possible to use an attenuator without any problems.

The volume control between the microphone pre-amplifier and the line amplifier controls the strength of the signal going to the record circuit. Therefore, if the recordist wants to record a loud sound, which would make the meter move to the right-hand end of the scale, the volume control has to be turned down thus reducing the strength of the signal going to the record circuit and therefore also the indication on the meter. It should be noted that the relationship between the meter and the record circuit remains constant and therefore, although the sound to be recorded may be louder than a man talking, it is conceivable that the recording may have the same strength. The volume control is like a tap, the function of which is to keep constant the flow of the water despite differing pressures in the supply.

The regulation of the volume control is made by the sound recordist according to the dictates of the conditions and the story of the film. On some tape recorders there are automatic volume controls. This is an amplifier which senses the volume of the sound signal coming from the microphone and adjusts the sensitivity of the microphone pre-amplifier accordingly. These amplifiers can be extremely complex and work very well, so that the untrained ear does not notice, but others are fierce in their action and the resultant sound hunts for the right level throughout the recording, with disconcerting results. The use of automatic volume controls should be avoided by the film sound recordist since there is no consistency in the recording level. This makes for difficulty in the sound editing and dubbing stages of film production, an aspect dealt with in a later chapter.

On some tape recorders, especially those designed for studio use, there is no

The tube contains a Cannon plug type insert at each end. There is space inside for the resistors needed for an attenuator.

Nagra 4.2 power supply. This device produces direct current to run the tape recorder, as well as 1 volt AC for pilot tone. It senses automatically the voltage of the mains and adjusts itself accordingly. Other power supplies have a voltage adjustment which should be set to the correct operating voltage before use.

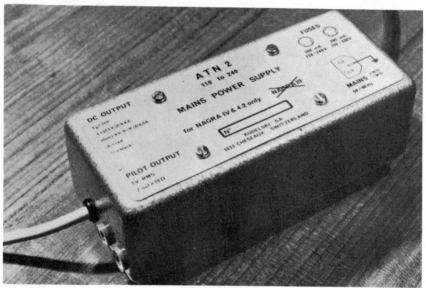

microphone pre-amplifier, because it is expected that the user will have such equipment in the studio mixing console. In portable tape recorders where it is convenient to have all the equipment in one package there is usually provision for changing the sensitivity of the mike input to line or zero level sensitivity, or there is a separate input, controlled by a separate volume control. The volume control sometimes also controls the strength of output from the recorder in replay. The line input, so-called to differentiate it from the microphone input, is designed to accept signals of around zero level (0dBm or about 0.7 volts) and is used when recording signals from other amplifiers such as record players, mixers, radios etc. In all probability the signal will be fed straight into the line amplifier in the recorder, as is the signal from the microphone pre-amplifier. The tape recorder will have a line output fed from the replay amplifier which will be suitable for feeding to the line input of other equipment.

There is usually the facility to turn the level meter into an indicator of the battery strength. The life of the batteries varies from recorder to recorder according to the size and number of batteries used, the amount of current the recorder takes, and whether the use of the batteries is intermittent or continuous. Rechargeable Nickel Cadmium cells can be used; the initial outlay is high, but with careful treatment such as never over-charging and never leaving discharged for a long time, the cells last far longer than the 100 chargings for which they are guaranteed. They are ideal for owner-operated equipment, but in hire equipment tend to be thrown away by recordists when they are flat. (I have a set of rechargeables which still perform perfectly more than 12 years after purchase.)

Portable tape recorders work from a *direct current* power supply. The batteries must be inserted in the correct direction so that the amplifier circuits are not damaged by current of the wrong polarity. There is usually a picture in the battery compartment showing the correct direction in which the battery should be pointing and sometimes the pins which make contact with the batteries are arranged so that mistakes are harder to make. Very great care must be taken when it is decided to power the recorder from another source to ensure that the current is (a) DC (b) of the right voltage, and (c) of the right polarity. It is advisable in those emergency situations when a motor car battery has to be used to have both a voltmeter and the instruction manual on hand before making connections.

There is usually an amplifier inside the recorder which regulates the voltage of the supply, so that although the batteries will discharge during use, the change in voltage will not affect the results obtained. It is usual for the motor of the recorder to be fed the unregulated voltage from the batteries when running fast forwards and backwards.

External power supplies are available for portable recorders so that they can be run from the mains. This power supply consists of a transformer to reduce the mains voltage to the low voltage required, and a rectifier which converts the AC into direct current.

Other Equipment in the Sound Recordist's Kit

Microphones

As has been seen there are several properties which prevail in the world of microphones: how they work, sensitivity, impedance, frequency response, and polar pattern. It is now necessary to examine the different types and the variations on the basic designs, and how they are used.

Getting rid of background noise is one of the most severe problems which the sound recordist has to face. The philosophy of recording must be that of recording the desired sound. Background noises being easy to add at a later stage. Two solutions exists for coping with background noise. Firstly, record in a quiet place, something that is not always possible but is always desirable, and which

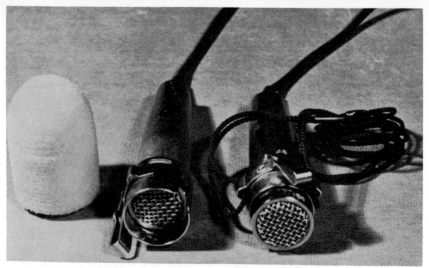

A pair of AKG D109 neck microphones. The foam windshield on the left is in fact a Dr. Scholes, toe cap. The clip around the end of the microphone can be moved. When it is in the position illustrated on the left hand microphone the frequency response illustrated in the graph below is obtained. Otherwise the microphone has a substantially flat frequency response.

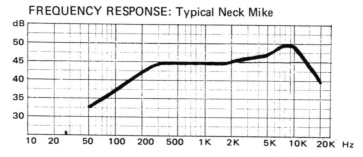

FREQUENCY RESPONSE: Typical Neck Mike

was dealt with in the grand manner by the first people to make sound films by building large studio complexes. In the absence of silence or a studio the solution lies in getting the microphone as close as possible to the sound that has to be recorded. One solution to this is the neck, chest or lavalier microphone.

As implied in its name the microphone is designed for use next to the chest of the person to be recorded; It must therefore be light in weight and small, so that it can be worn underneath clothing without causing a bulge, or concealed behind a tie. It has to be designed with a frequency response curve which compensates for the close proximity of the chest barrel. In the diagram of the frequency response curve it can be seen that such microphones tend to have a reduced bass response and a characteristic peak in the response in the region of 6- to 7KHz. Sound picked up from the region of the chest has a boomy quality caused by the resonance of the chest and the fact that the microphone is not in

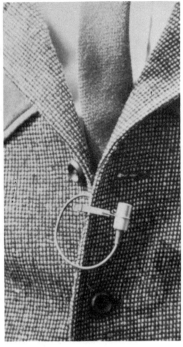

A Sony ECM50 in use. Top left: *Double-sided sticky tape used to hold the microphone in place behind a lapel. It is difficult to get rid of the noise from clothing but this is a useful way of concealing the microphone. If possible the end of the microphone should be left open to the air to prevent the sound becoming too muffled. The other two photographs illustrate the use of clips supplied with the microphone.*

the direct path of the sounds made by the lips and the tongue. The frequency response for neck microphones compensates adequately and the sound obtained is quite natural. There are some problems about using these microphones. The position of the microphone is static relative to the body and therefore there is no possibility of adding perspective to the sound obtained. The results obtained are satisfactory as long as the actor does not turn his head to one side, when the sound changes radically.

The fact that the microphone is hidden under clothing affects the frequency response differently according to the clothing, which if it is heavy reduces the upper frequency response alarmingly. If the actor moves his hands to his chest or face there is a sharp change in the sound quality caused by the reflection of the sound waves by the hand. The microphone is usually very sensitive to movement of clothing against it. For this there are a few solutions. Normally the microphone is supplied with a lanyard which can be hung around the neck of the actor, unless there is a need for speed in operation it is probably best to ignore this and use wide adhesive tape for securing the microphone either to the skin or the inside of the clothes of the actor. Some recordists devise belts which can

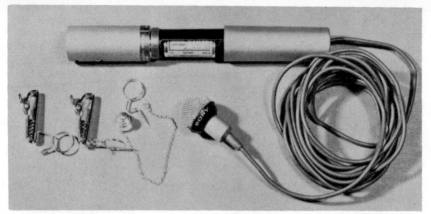

The Sony ECM50 microphone, showing the three separate clips and the wind-shield (on the microphone). The power supply, which is at the other end of the microphone lead, unscrews for the battery to be inserted. This lasts for several thousand hours and should be replaced about every four months.

be tied around the chest of the actor which perform the same function with greater comfort.

Most neck microphones are moving-coil and omni-directional. New designs coming out seem to favour capacitor operation. The result is an extremely small microphone which is attached by cable to a power pack and amplifier module. Some of the designs have used a new kind of capacitor called an *electret*. This capacitor is permanently charged and therefore does not need a polarising voltage, considerable power savings being made in this way, and a small battery in the amplifier will last several months.

At least one neck microphone has been designed so that the characteristic frequency response is obtained by attaching the lanyard sleeve and thus it is possible to change the microphone into a fairly normal one for use in emergencies.

Neck microphones are frequently used in conjunction with wireless or radio transmitters, when they become called wireless or radio microphones. This system removes the need for microphone cables leading from the actor to the tape recorder and allows considerable mobility. At the tape recorder there is a receiver which plugs into the normal microphone input. The frequency band allocated in Britain has proved suitable for two radio mikes to be used simultaneously without interaction, which manifests itself as a whistle heard on the audio signal. The range of the transmitter is affected by the nature of the terrain, which in cities is limited to the line of sight by the presence of reinforced concrete structures, interference from electrical systems such as motor car ignitions, and powerful other transmitters such as those used by the police. Many designs are available and increasing sophistication is the order of the day. In the transmitter of one design there is a two-light meter which enables the operator to set the volume accurately, coupled with this is a sophisticated automatic volume control which prevents distortion. Furthermore the transmitter is designed to provide power for a number of different types of condenser microphone. At the receiver

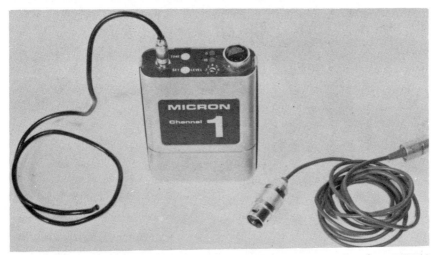

Above: *Micron Wireless Microphone transmitter, showing aerial and an ECM50 microphone. There are two buttons, one for tone, the other to activate a two-light meter (marked 0 and −10). The screw hole with numbers around it is the microphone volume control. Care should be taken to use the screw-driver provided, since it is easy to damage the head of this screw.* Below: *The receiver for a Micron wireless microphone. As can be seen from the cover this contains many facilities for the sound recordist, giving information about the receiver and transmitter at the flick of a switch.*

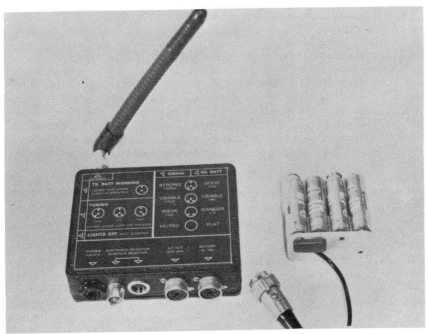

there is a sophisticated indication of the signal strength being received and the operator can tell at all times whether the system is operating correctly. There is also a warning light in the receiver which flashes about half an hour before the batteries in the transmitter are about to fail. The transmitter and the receiver are switched on by attaching the connecting plugs.

Radio microphones are being used in *cinéma verité* situations where the action is unpredictable but the need exists for recording the sound. They are also used in television studios for discussion programmes and musical shows where the use of a mike with a cable is impracticable.

The main problems are of possible interaction between transmitters, interference from external electrical sources, signal fading in built-up areas, and the fact that a neck mike is usually used. Nevertheless radio microphones are being used more frequently than ever before as the more adventurous film-makers find subjects which are suited to their use.

Ultra-Directional Microphones

Sound waves are reflected by objects with dimensions greater than the wavelength of the sound, in other words a circle of metal or wood with a diameter of 3 feet (0.91m) will reflect sounds with that wavelength (375Hz) and shorter (higher frequencies). The same applies to a tube, therefore we can make a tube resonate at a frequency whose wavelength is related to the length of the tube.

This preamble is to highlight the problems confronting the microphone designer trying to make the sound equivalent of a telescopic lens. The optical engineer is dealing with a medium which has extremely short wavelengths. His problem is light-gathering and he goes to great lengths to achieve this—200 inch (5m) reflectors in telescopes. But the large telescopes are built that way because they need to be very sensitive to light. The acoustic engineer needs to design large reflectors to gather sound and focus the waves only because of the wavelengths involved.

There are two approaches to the ultra-directional microphone. One is to take a circular reflector with a parabolic profile, and place a microphone (omni-directional) at the point of focus. The reflector concentrates the sound waves at the microphone. But frequencies with a wavelength which is longer than the diameter of the reflector are not reflected. However, if the reflector (or dish, as it is often called) is three feet in diameter it will reflect all sounds (and therefore be directional) above the frequency of 375Hz. Reflectors are sometimes provided with a tripod and sights, and have the advantage of being cheap, although bulky.

Since most of the sounds for which such devices are needed, such as speech and animal sounds, have basic frequency ranges which are higher, ultra-directional microphones do not have to be too large. Background sounds with a lower frequency can be filtered out either while recording or at a later stage.

The other method of making ultra-directional microphones depends on a resonant tube, or series of tubes. Traditionally tube microphones, called gun or rifle microphones, were made as a cluster of about 50 fine tubes, each one different in length, with a microphone transducer placed at one end, the other ends being open. Sound arriving along the axis of the tubes travels down all the tubes and arrives at the transducer in step. Sound arriving from the side also travels down all the tubes but, because of the different distances the sound waves

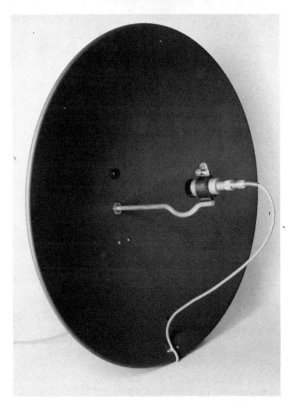

A parabolic reflector made by Grampian.   Photo: *Grampian Reproducers Ltd.*

have to travel, arrives out of phase at the transducer, thus cancelling itself out. The microphone is therefore sensitive to sounds coming from one end only, and displays a rapidly diminishing sensitivity to sounds coming from the sides. The directional properties hold true for sound waves which have a wavelength twice the length of the tubes. Similar in design is the current trend in ultra-directional microphones. They consist of a single tube, with a series of openings along one side, and lined with a graded acoustic impedance made of felt. This acoustic impedance is the crucial part of the design of such microphones because it allows a predominance of a particular frequency to enter the tube only at a point along the length of the tube which will ensure its arrival at the transducer out of phase with the sound wave of a similar frequency which has travelled down the whole length of the tube.

Rifle microphones are expensive. They are very directional and must be aimed with care. Their use indoors can be dangerous if the acoustics of the room are bad, since they pick up not only the sound of the actors but also the sound reflected from walls, and this can produce drastic changes in the environmental quality of the sound when the microphone is favoured from one direction to another.

A parabolic reflector works in much the same way as a reflecting telescope. The wavelength of the sound waves dictates, however, that the reflector diameter be large in order to reflect the lowest frequencies.

Microphone Windshields

In windy conditions out of doors and when the microphone is moved quickly or used for close speech recording indoors, microphones become almost impossible to use without some protection from moving masses of air. The device used, called a windshield, wind gag or pop shield, has to stop the movement of large quantities of air and yet allow the sound waves to reach the microphone. There are two main methods of construction:

(1) A framework of wire or plastics supports a fine cloth or foam which surrounds the microphone.

(2) A foam plastic, called acoustifoam, is shaped so that it can be secured around the microphone. Acoustifoam consists not of little spheres of plastics but of tubes which allow the passage of sound waves.

Generally the larger the windshield the more effective it is. Indeed some can be used in very strong winds. In the design of windshields care has to be taken that the frequency response of the microphone is not adversely affected. For this reason it is not advisable to make windshields oneself except in emergencies. Sometimes one can effectively shield a microphone with one's body. I have a woollen cap which is very effective against wind and does not seem to affect the quality of the sound too much. The addition of a woman's stocking to the kit is helpful, since it will fit well over a rifle microphone windshield and gives a little more protection in severe wind. The point is that if a windshield is not available a loss of sound quality can be accepted in order to obtain a recording which is not ruined by wind noise.

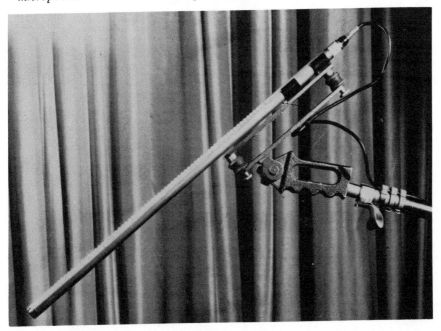

L = Low Pressure
H = High Pressure

Above: *The sounds picked up from the direction of the end of the tube arrive at the diaphragm in phase. This ensures their dominance over sounds arriving at the side, which are out of phase.* Below: *A Sennheiser MKH805 rifle microphone and shock mounted pistol grip.*

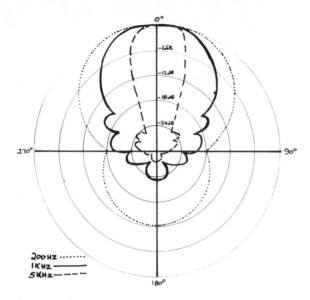

Polar diagram: rifle microphone.

Rifle microphone windshield. This surrounds the microphone with still air, preventing wind noise.

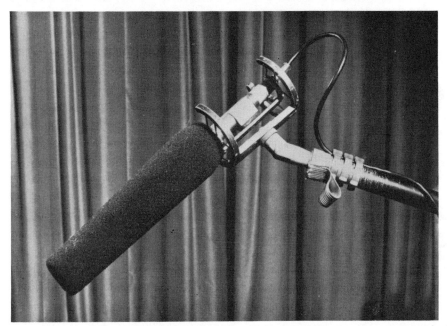

Above: *Foam plastic windshield on a Sennheiser MKH415. This type of wind-shield is not very effective outdoors but will prevent rumble from a microphone which is being moved quickly, and will stop 'popping' if the microphone is used close to the mouth. Note that the microphone is suspended in a cradle which is isolated from the boom by elastic. Below: MKH415 inside a wind-shield, suspended by elastic. The windshield is made of plastic lined with fine cloth.*

The complete windshield.

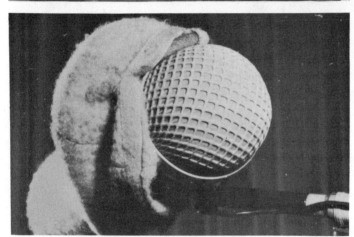

The complete windshield with outer covering, which prevents the wind whistling in the support material, being fitted.

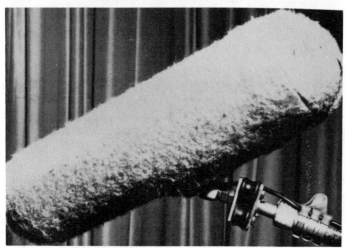

Sometimes it is necessary to add a flexible shock mount between the windshield and the boom to prevent handling noises reaching the microphone.

The author on an oil rig wearing protective clothing, a hard hat, a Nagra, headphones and a rifle microphone. Note how the headphones have been turned through 90° so that they can be worn in spite of the hat. The Nagra is always slung on the right side of the body so that the controls can be operated without obscuring the meter. This more or less dictates that the microphone is held in the left hand.

Microphones: Other Noises

When physically handling microphones it is possible that vibrations from the hands or the stand on which the microphone is placed will cause vibrations which can be transmitted through the microphone casing to the diaphragm of the microphone. These noises are unacceptable since they are unexplained by any action on the picture. Therefore it is necessary to take precautions that they do not happen.

Hand Holding Microphones

Take care when holding a microphone in the hand that it is well gripped by the fingers. Once recording the fingers must not be moved since the movement can cause vibrations which will be heard as very loud scraping noises. It is important to see that the plug at the back of the microphone is securely fastened, if necessary by using adhesive tape, since movement of the microphone can cause the plug to move relatively producing thumps on the recording. An extra precaution in this case is to hold the cable in a loop alongside the microphone. It is advisable in the case of microphones which have a series of holes down the side of the casing (part of the acoustic labyrinth which makes it directional) to be sure that the holes are left uncovered by the hand.

Left: *a commercially available microphone thread adaptor.* Right: *a home-made adaptor, made from light fittings, just as effective and one quarter the price.*

Above: *Commercially made thread adaptors.* Below: *The home-made alternative. Much cheaper, but the smaller one has to be tapped with a ⅜ths Whitworth tap.*

Using Microphones with Stands and Booms

It is convenient when recording music and dialogue to mount the microphone on a stand or microphone boom. There is however the need to isolate the microphone from any vibrations which may be transmitted through floor stands or created by the handling of booms. Microphone suspensions or shock mounts are used. These consist of a screw thread which goes on to the stand

A fishpole in operation. The sound recordist is well out of the way on dry land. Photo: John Dixon.

or boom, and a clip for holding the microphone which is isolated from the rest through elastic supports usually made of rubber or neoprene.

Microphone Stands

There are many types of microphone floor stand. The main point about such stands is that they should be stable, since their use implies that the microphone is to be left unattended. This means either that the stand should be heavy at the base or that the base, if it consists of three feet, should have a good spread. When using a microphone on a stand make sure that the cable is firmly secured to the bottom of the stand since this allows less leverage to pull the stand over if anyone should trip over the cable. Be sure that the cable is out of the way and does not run the risk of being tripped over.

Microphone Booms

There are two types of microphone boom, the hand boom known as a fish pole, and the studio boom. The fish pole is constructed of light-weight metal tubing which can telescope to provide lengths of anything from about 4 to 14 feet (1.22m to 4.3m). Some are made of fibre-glass tubing. At the full extension the fish pole should not have too much 'whip'. The microphone can be mounted on the end of the pole with an ordinary shock mount or sometimes on a device hanging down from the end which enables the microphone to be favoured when

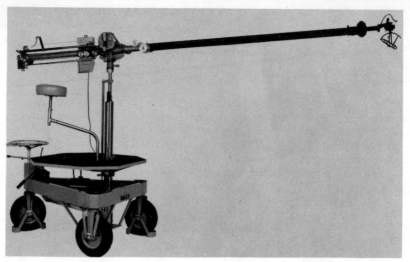

A Fisher boom. This type of boom is mainly used in the studio.

Photo: J. L. Fisher Inc.

the pole is twisted. It is more usual to favour the microphone by simply twisting the pole. The cable from the microphone is secured at the end of the pole with adhesive tape or a clip and the cable then wrapped around the pole snake fashion down to the operator (boom swinger).

The studio boom is a complex affair consisting of a trolley on which is mounted a pedestal which carries a counterweighted boom. A cat's cradle of strings and pulleys enables the boom to be racked in and out, and the microphone on the end to be favoured both sideways and vertically. The boom (jib) can be swung radially and vertically. This device is probably the most flexible way of getting a microphone close in on a scene.

Attenuators and other In-Line Plugs

Attenuators are used when it is necessary to reduce the strength of the signal from a microphone. It is usual to construct them inside a tube which has a pair of opposite cannon plugs at each end. Such tubes are available but if unobtainable two cannon plugs screwed together back to back do the job just as well. There are formulae for working out the values of the resistances needed for a given amount of attenuation. The circuit is:

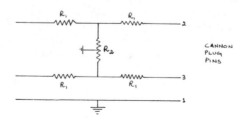

The values for the resistors in the circuit for 200 Ω and 50 Ω microphones are as follows:

	200 Ω		50 Ω	
	R$_1$	R$_2$	R$_1$	R$_2$
10dB	52	140	13	35
15dB	70	73	17	18
20dB	82	40	20	10
25dB	89	23	22	6

The resistors should be of high quality but need only be 1/4 watt. This means that they will be small and therefore not too difficult to fit inside the connector.

Attenuators should not be used between a condenser microphone and its power pack, or between a condenser microphone power pack and the tape recorder if the power pack has a built-in bass cut. There are power packs available which apply 20dB of attenuation to the signal from the microphone.

In the same type of connecting tube it is possible to make a straight connection between the pins of the plugs. However if the signal carrying pins are reversed so that the phase of the microphone can be changed then it is possible by inserting the connector in a microphone line to either reverse the phase of the microphone or, in the event of a condenser microphone not working because the cable is incorrectly connected for power, inserting the phase reverser will apply the right correction.

There are times when inadequate cables make it very useful to have a plug sex reverser. This consists of a tube with the same type of plug insert in each end, either female or male.

Two cannon plugs fitted back to back to make a sex changer for microphone leads.

Mixers

A mixer allows the recordist to combine the signals from several microphones into one output, with individual control over the signal of each microphone. There are occasions when it is necessary to use more than one microphone either to capture dialogue which originates from widely spaced places in the picture, or when recording music.

Mixers for studio use are very complex and will be dealt with in another chapter. To save weight mixers for portable tape recorders are kept simple. They consist of a series of microphone pre-amplifiers which are fed via a series of volume controls into a line amplifier and from there into the line input of the tape recorder. This means that the line volume control of the tape recorder will become a master volume control for all the microphone inputs on the mixer. Facilities for tone control vary. Almost without exception separate bass cut circuits are available on each channel (microphone input). Sometimes treble and bass tone controls are available for the whole output of the mixer or one channel, and occasionally one finds a mixer which has separate treble and bass controls for each channel. As the complexity increases so does the weight and cost of the mixer. Some mixers will provide phantom powering for condenser microphones, as well as up to 60dB of attenuation on each channel. The mixer may have a meter but it is perfectly possible to use the meter on the tape recorder. If the meter on the mixer is to be used then it is important to line it up to the meter on the tape recorder otherwise one could over- or under-record. To do this tone must be fed into an input in the mixer (if the mixer has not already got a tone generator) and both meters adjusted so that they read the same value.

The Rest of the Kit

It will be seen from the preceding pages that the sound recordist's kit is quite complex, and that there is a large variety of equipment which can be included. There is a basic kit which fulfils most of the needs for almost all jobs. Some hire companies actually rent out the equipment as a basic kit but they are few and far between. Mostly it is only possible to hire a tape recorder and a couple of microphones, the rest being extra hire. Some sound recordists prefer to own the basic kit of equipment and then hire in the extra items as they are needed. One of the advantages of hiring equipment is that the hire company usually keeps a close check on the condition and performance of the equipment and are also obliged to keep spare equipment on hand to cover the recordist in the event of equipment going wrong. Sound equipment which is not maintained properly is distressing for the recordist since even by the feel of the controls it is easy to lose confidence. A sound recordist must have confidence in his equipment.

An ideal basic sound recordist's kit might be:

Portable tape recorder.
Headphones.
Condenser cardioid microphone.
Moving coil cardioid microphone.
Omni-directional microphone.
a Pair of neck microphones.
Power supply for the condenser microphone.

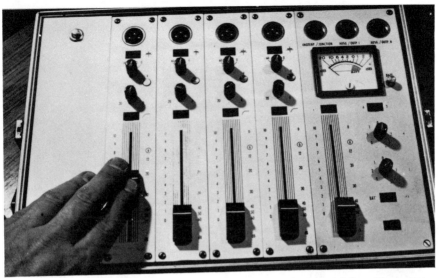

A Sennheiser portable microphone mixer suitable for use with a Nagra tape recorder.

Spare batteries for the recorder and the microphone.
Microphone cables.
Attenuator.
Windshields for the microphones.
Mains power supply for the recorder.
Mixer and the cable to connect it to the recorder.

It would be nice to see a rifle microphone as a normal part of the kit but it is so expensive an item that it is usually hired as an extra. Sometimes one finds a separate pre-amplifier supplied with the kit. This plugs into the accessory socket of the recorder and turns the line input into a microphone input. It is a very convenient device for its use often means that a mixer is not necessary, thus saving both weight and money.

There are a number of other items which sometimes make life as a sound recordist easier. The sort of thing I am thinking of is the silk stocking which one can include in the kit as an extra protection against wind. A material called "Blu-Stik" which is used in offices for sticking charts onto the wall, a sort of plasticine which does not leave a mark behind but is adhesive, can be used for sticking a small microphone to a wall easily. A ball of strong nylon fishing line is useful if the need arises for suspending a microphone between two points. A supply of rubber bands never ceases to be useful.

Then there is a kit of tools for on-the-job maintenance of equipment. This can consist of a small number of items. I favour screwdrivers which have separate blades which can be slotted into the handle. There are some which have a small torch in the handle. Apart from big screwdrivers there is a need for the small type used by watch makers. A vice grip doubles as a pair of pliers and a spanner,

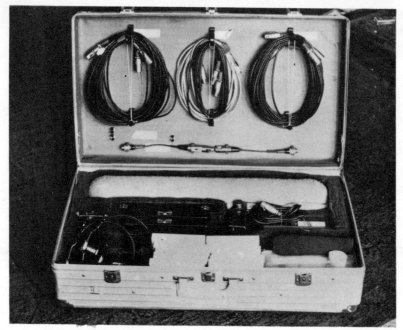

Above: *Suitcase containing most of the equipment needed for sound recording. In the lid there is a supply of cables, and the body of the case contains microphones, windshields, suspensions and tape.* Below: *A Nagra microphone preamplifier can be plugged into the accessory socket to convert the line input of the recorder into a microphone input. This means that three microphones can be used with the Nagra IV and to a large extent makes a mixer unnecessary.*

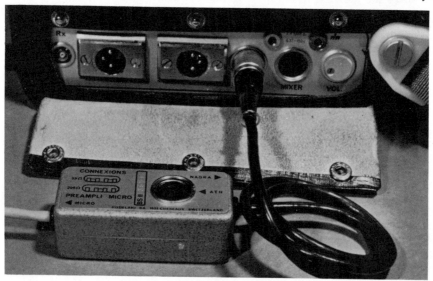

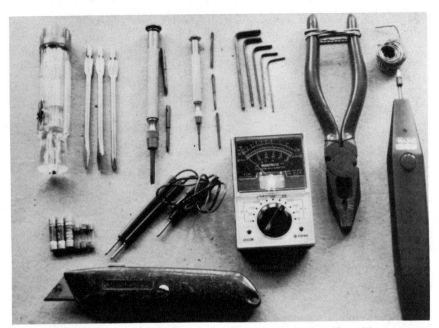

A basic maintenance kit. Top left: *screwdrivers of varying sizes.* Top centre: *Allen keys (metric).* Bottom left: *fuses and Stanley knife.* Centre: *small meter.* Right: *pliers, battery soldering iron and solder.*

and since it is possible to clamp them, they are very useful for holding plugs while soldering. A pair of wire cutters (side cutters) is vital, as is a sharp knife (I prefer a retractable Stanley knife.) Spare fuses for the tape recorder power supply and mains plugs are useful. A small meter which will measure voltages and resistance is quite important. It is important to have a soldering iron and if it is possible this should be able to be run off batteries. There are rechargeable battery soldering irons now available which will cope with completely desoldering and resoldering about three cannon plugs on one charge. Then there are such items as glue, pins, paper clips, pencils and pens which may come in useful at times. Facetious as it may sound perhaps the most useful item in such a kit is a bottle opener—it will save the crew on many an occasion.

That more or less concludes the sound recordist's basic kit and how it works.

There is one important aspect of recording which has been missed out so far and that is the synchronisation of the camera and the tape recorder for synchronous sound shooting. Therefore before examining how the equipment is used, the next chapter will be about synchronisation.

Close up of the parts of a Westrex Film Recorder. A: Drive sprocket. B: Spring-loaded rollers which keep the film tensioned. C: Capstans, connected to flywheels behind the deck plate. D: Erase head. E: Record head. F: Replay head.

Chapter IV

Synchronous Sound Recording

The Magnetic Film Recorder

The tape recorder provides a convenient way of recording sound tracks for films. It is, however, almost impossible to use tape for the later processes of film production, such as editing and dubbing, because of difficulties in synchronisation. The sound track recorded on tape is therefore transferred to magnetic film. Historically, in the development of the sound techniques which we use to-day, sound track production started on disc for such Warner Brother classics as *The Singing Fool* and *The Jazz Singer*. The editing and dubbing processes were extremely difficult. When separate sound tracks were recorded photographically the advantages were immediately apparent, and there was a rapid switch to the new system. There is little electronic difference between the magnetic tape recorder and the magnetic film recorder. There is, however, a mechanical and philosophical difference which should be examined in detail.

The essence of synchronisation between two pieces of film is that they both run at the same speed from the same starting point. The illustration of a synchroniser (on page 154), a device used in the editing process for running two pieces of film in synchronism, shows what I mean. The film is locked onto the teeth of the sprockets with guides. The sprockets are on the same shaft and therefore when one piece of film moves the other must also. It is therefore easy to synchronise separate pieces of film whether they be picture or sound. (The intricacies of this synchronisation will be examined later in this chapter.)

The magnetic film recorder uses film coated with magnetic iron oxide, and which has the same dimensions as photographic film in either 16mm or 35mm. In order to take advantage of the ease of synchronisation afforded by the perforations in the film, it is driven by a sprocket. This introduces a problem. The teeth of the sprocket do not drive the film at a constant speed. As they engage and disengage with the perforations they impart a ripple to the motion of the film. In order to smooth out this ripple the film is wrapped around (usually) two capstans which are attached to flywheels. The film drives these flywheels, which, because of the momentum built up, iron out the ripple. To keep the film tight around the capstans there are two spring-loaded rollers, which are damped by a small shock-absorber called a *dashpot*, and which prevents the rollers from oscillating to and fro.

This simplified description should highlight the difference between a tape recorder and a film recorder. The tape recorder drives the tape at a constant speed but is difficult to synchronise because the tape can slip, expand or contract or stretch, and the capstan changes size with temperature and wear. On the other hand the film recorder drives the film positively and synchronously via the perforations, but wow and flutter-free recordings can only be achieved by the use of passive capstans and flywheels which absorb the ripple imparted to the movement of the film by the sprocket.

The front panel of a Westrex Film Recorder, showing the film path.

The sprocket is driven by a motor. This is usually a synchronous motor which has the property of running at a speed which is directly proportional to the frequency of the mains current. The gearing of the motor will be such as to drive the film at 24 frames per second, and it may well be supplied with a

The back of an RCA film recorder showing the flywheels and the motor.

gearbox which allows for 25 fps as well. There is usually a separate motor for take up and feed. These can be used for fast winding the film provided it is taken out of the sprocket and flywheel assembly.

The fact that the film is driving the capstans makes for start-up characteristics which are different to those of an ordinary tape recorder. The flywheels are heavy and it takes a while for the film to drive them up to the correct speed. On modern machines this will take about 5 seconds. This means that it is necessary to wait some 5 seconds for the sprung rollers to settle before starting a recording if wow and flutter at the beginning are to be avoided. There are machines available which have a motor which drives the flywheels while the film is stationary and therefore the start up time is reduced. It will be apparent from the description that the film recorder has to be a heavy piece of equipment, solidly constructed. Portable models are available. They run on a car battery and can easily be used on location when the need for mobility does not exist. The film which is recorded should however be transferred to another film as a safety measure. This aspect does not arise when tape is used for the master recording since a transfer is necessary anyway.

Recording Synchronous Sound

Initially it is necessary to consider synchronous sound recording on film. The essence of the process is that the film containing the picture should run at exactly the same speed as the film containing the sound. During the recording process this is all that is needed. At a later stage, in reproduction, it is important that the two media, picture and sound, run not only at the same speed but in step from the start to the finish.

There are two basic sub-groups for recording synchronous sound: *single-system and double-system.*

Single-System Sound Recording

In single-system sound recording the film which is being used for recording the picture is also used to record the sound (in video-tape recording the same applies). The advantages and disadvantages will become apparent.

It is important to realise the difference between picture and sound recording. Picture is recorded intermittently while for sound recording the film must be running at as constant a speed as possible. This means that the recording of the picture and the sound cannot take place at the same place on the film. There has to be a physical separation between the picture and the sound for the same instant in time. There are standards which regulate this separation:

	Optical	Magnetic
16mm	26 frames advanced	28 frames advanced
35mm	19½ frames advanced	28 frames retarded

Single system sound is generally only used for news recording with 16mm cameras. The cameras have therefore to be lightweight. But in order to construct a mechanism which will run film sound at a constant speed let alone iron out the intermittent motion of the picture mechanism heavy flywheels are needed. These would add too much weight to a hand-held camera, and a compromise needs to be worked out. This is based on the needs for the camera which are generally those of recording speech and effects. If music is to be recorded then it is necessary to go to much greater lengths for the recording anyway. Therefore the smoothing mechanism for the sound in a single system camera is designed to give results good enough for the clear recording of speech. It is possible to use a small flywheel or friction smoothing in the camera and achieve adequate results. It is important to have a good motor in the camera which will not impart wow to the recording by virtue of variable speed running. Traditionally

16mm Arriflex BL camera fitted with a single-system module. This contains a flywheel and rollers which stabilise the movement of the film, and record (a) and replay (b) heads.

single system sound was recorded using a photographic process. The grain structure of picture film is too coarse for good recording and the sound track is now recorded on a strip of magnetic iron oxide which is coated down the side of the picture.

Editing the film presents problems since whenever the picture is cut so is the sound track, and because of the separation between the picture and the sound the cut is right for one of the two only. This is not too serious for newsreel material where the original material is usually televised, and the immediacy of the content usually transcends the slight crudity in the editing. For work where it is necessary to have a print anyway, such as documentaries, the sound track will have to be transferred to another piece of film. This involves the master picture film in the slight extra risk of scratching during the transfer process. On the other hand there is no delay between development and projection since the sound track is fixed to the film and the synchronisation remains constant, thus saving an editing process. The use of single system makes filming much simpler because there is only one piece of equipment involved.

Inside the camera there are usually two heads, record and replay. The assumption is made that since the stock is fresh there is no need for an erase head. A separate amplifier is connected to the camera. This amplifier has its own batteries which ensure that the sound recordist can monitor regardless of whether the camera is on or off. Whenever the amplifier is plugged in and switched on there is bias applied to the record head. It is imperative that before unplugging the amplifier from the camera, the amplifier is switched off. If this is not done there is a good chance that the record head in the camera may become magnetised

The amplifier pack for a single-system Arriflex BL. This pack has a meter, headphone output and provision for two microphones.

as a result of the bias signal being at peak strength at the instant of disconnection.

Double-System Sound

In double-system sound recording the sound is recorded on a separate piece of film (or tape) to the picture. Synchronisation of the two pieces of film now relies on the ability of the equipment to run them at exactly the same speed. It is perhaps safer to say "at exactly the same number of frames per second" since there is no reason why a picture recorded on 35mm film should not be run synchronously with a 16mm sound track. Although the linear speed of the two will be different by virtue of their different dimensions they can be synchronised easily if they run at the same number of frames per second.

Synchronisation can be achieved electrically or mechanically. It is well to note that the methods used in camera/sound recorder set-ups do not differ much from those used in the dubbing theatre.

Double-System Sound—Mechanical Synchronisation (no longer in use)

Built into one camera mechanism are separate heads, one for picture and one for sound. Essentially a camera and a magnetic film recorder are clamped together and driven by a common motor. Since the two mechanisms are driven in this way it is easy to ensure that both the picture film and the sound film run at the same speed. Such cameras have existed but suffer from being too heavy.

Double-System Sound—Electrical Synchronisation

The camera with a built-in sound recorder (double-system camera with mechanical interlock) is too heavy. If the two devices, the camera and the magnetic film recorder, can be separated, a more versatile outfit can be made. The only way to do this is to use an electrical system of synchronisation. The solution lies in the use of the three-phase synchronous motor. As said before these motors run at a speed defined by the frequency of the current driving them. If two synchronous motors are run from the same three-phase current source then they will run at the same speed provided that they are not expected to drive equipment with too great a load, and that the voltage of the supply is sufficient. It is sometimes a problem to find the correct three-phase supply, especially on location, and it may be necessary to provide a generator of some kind. Two devices are important in the powering of three-phase synchronous motors when a three-phase supply is not available. Firstly the phase splitter, which takes a single phase supply and by a network of capacitors delays the current from the single phase sufficiently to create a three-phase supply. The phase splitter has to be designed for a specific motor and the load expected of the motor. The other device needed when there is no supply available is an inverter. This converts the direct current from a low-voltage motor car battery into alternating current at approximately the correct frequency and at the right voltage. The addition of a phase splitter will complete the circuit and enable the camera and the film recorder to be driven at the same speed provided they are fitted with synchronous motors.

It should be mentioned that since there is a very marked difference in frequency standards between the U.S.A. and Canada and some other countries and the rest of the world—60Hz and 50Hz—motors designed to work on one frequency will operate at a different speed when operated on the other frequency. It should be noted that the speed of two 50Hz synchronous motors running on 60Hz will still be the same, but instead of running at 1500rpm for instance they would run at 1800rpm. In other words the speed of the motor is directly proportional to the frequency of the current driving it and thus would be no good for filming, because the speed would be wrong although still in synchronisation.

There is one major difference between the mechanical double-system and single-system, and the electrical systems. Single-system and mechanical double-system produce a sound record which is synchronised frame-for-frame with the whole roll of picture. Therefore with the mechanical double system all it is necessary to do in order to re-establish synchronisation after the picture has been processed is to mark both the picture and the sound before shooting at a convenient place such as the picture gate and the record head. These can then be lined up at a later stage in the same heads on a double-headed projector prior to presentation.

With electrical interlock between the camera and the magnetic film recorder, relying on synchronous motors, there is no guarantee that both the camera and the film recorder will run up to operating speed in step with each other, and therefore any marks placed on the films will not necessarily be a mark of synchronisation. It is also possible that the sound recorder may be started before the camera because of the greater time needed for the speed to stabilise and the fact that the sound film stock is cheaper than the photographic stock. So, it is only when the motors of both machines are running at their operating speed that there is a guarantee that they are running at the same speed and therefore only then that it is safe to add synchronisation marks. It is for this reason that the film industry has adopted the ubiquitous clapper board. When the stick on the clapper board is clapped down on to the board itself, a record of exact synchronisation is provided that an editor can easily use.

Double-System Sound—Film for Picture, Tape for Sound

The mobility of the film unit was severely limited until the arrival of the lightweight portable tape recorder in the late 1950's, and a system for reliable synchronisation between it and the camera. A special note should be made of the Leevers-Rich Synchro Pulse system which was introduced in about 1950. The recorder was contained in two heavy boxes, the recorder and its amplifier, and for power used a large 12 volt heavy duty lorry battery. This recorder replaced the optical sound camera and the truck that housed it and was therefore a tremendous step towards portability. Hardly however the type of machine which we are used to to-day, which can easily be slung over the shoulder.

In effect, all systems so far designed to synchronise the camera and the tape recorder, use a tape recorder which runs at a standard speed and records data on the tape of the speed of the camera film. This means that it does not really matter what the speed of the tape is. Transfer of the tape to film is the crucial

A clapper board.

process, and one which is necessary anyway so that the editor can easily match the picture film to the sound film.

Recording the Synchronising Signal

It is more or less universal to use a variant of a system invented in the early 1950's called *pilot tone*. I shall use the term pilot tone frequently but want to make it clear that this trade name has come to be used as the generic term for synchronising systems.

A synchronous motor runs at a speed defined by the frequency of the mains current which is driving it. The reverse applies. An alternator, which is an

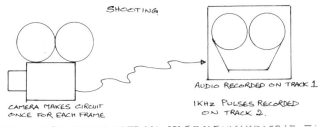

SHOOTING

AUDIO RECORDED ON TRACK 1

CAMERA MAKES CIRCUIT
ONCE FOR EACH FRAME

1KHz PULSES RECORDED
ON TRACK 2.

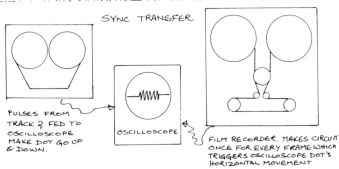

SYNC TRANSFER

PULSES FROM
TRACK 2 FED TO
OSCILLOSCOPE
MAKE DOT GO UP
& DOWN.

OSCILLOSCOPE

FILM RECORDER MAKES CIRCUIT
ONCE FOR EVERY FRAME WHICH
TRIGGERS OSCILLOSCOPE DOT'S
HORIZONTAL MOVEMENT

PROVIDING THE PULSE REMAINS STATIONARY THE TAPE &
FILM ARE IN SYNCHRONISM. THE SPEED OF THE TAPE IS VARIED
TO KEEP THE PULSE STILL.

alternating current generator, generates an alternating current which has a frequency proportional to the speed at which the alternator is being turned. A small alternator is fitted to the camera mechanism and geared so that it will generate a specific frequency when the camera is running at a certain speed. The voltage of the generator is usually in the region of 1 volt. For the sake of this book the camera speed and frequency which has the easiest mathematical relationship will be used, i.e. a camera speed of 25 frames per second and a frequency of 50Hz. It is a good idea to note that there are three ratios between the camera speed and pilot tone frequency in use. They are:

25fps	50Hz	100Hz	(TV film speed except the 60Hz countries)
24fps	50Hz	100Hz	(Cinema film speed)
24fps	60Hz		(60Hz countries)

Frequencies in the third column are double those in the second and apply in limited degree to Perfectone equipment. In countries where there is 60Hz mains there is no dual standard for film used in television, and therefore only one ratio is shown.

The frequency of the output of the alternator is proportional to the speed at which the alternator is being driven, and is therefore proportional to the speed of the camera. Thus if the camera speed to frequency ratio is 25fps:50Hz, should the camera be running at the wrong speed, say 24fps, the frequency of the output of the alternator, the pilot tone, will be proportionately different, i.e. 48Hz. This frequency will then be recorded on the tape. For the moment, however, it is best to look at a straight-forward example where everything is

99

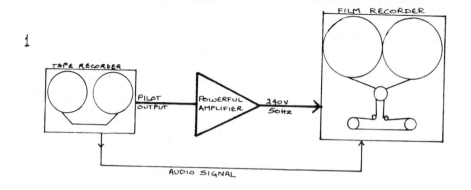

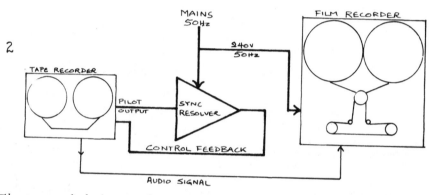

The two methods for transferring ¼ inch tape to film using pilot tone to maintain synchronism.

running correctly. The ratio is 25fps:50Hz, and the speed of the tape is exactly 7.5ips (19.05 cm/s). In order to obtain a transfer of the tape to film which will synchronise with the film which ran through the camera, the magnetic film recorder has to run at 25fps and the tape at exactly 7.5ips (19.05 cm/s). It is easy to construct a film recorder which will run at 25fps when it is driven by a synchronous motor running from 50Hz mains supply. The problem lies in getting the tape to run at the right speed, since there are so many variables such as tape slip and shrinkage which can come into play. Only by referring to the pilot tone recorded on the tape can synchronous replay be achieved.

There are two ways of using pilot tone. Firstly, a powerful amplifier amplifies the pilot tone signal coming off the tape, and converts it into three phase current at the right voltage. This current is used to drive the motor in the magnetic film recorder. Since the motor is synchronous, it will drive the film recorder at a speed proportional to the frequency of the current which is driving it. Therefore the speed of the film recorder will be determined by the frequency of the pilot tone from the replay tape recorder. It will be noted that the

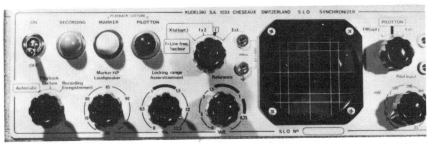

A Nagra SLO synchroniser, which controls the speed of the Nagra in play-back by comparing the frequency of the pilot tone on the tape with that of the mains.

relationship of the frequency that drives the film recorder to the speed at which it is running is the same as that used in the camera.

In the case of the camera that was running at 24fps and producing 48Hz the replay machine will produce a pilot tone frequency of 48Hz (assuming that it is running at exactly 7.5ips (19.05 cm/s) which will drive the magnetic film recorder at 24fps also. There is therefore an exact duplication of the speed at which the camera ran. It does not matter whether the variation in the speed comes in the replay tape recorder. The important thing is that the ratio between the camera speed and the frequency of the pilot tone is being duplicated in transfer.

In the second system the magnetic film recorder is run on the three-phase mains power supply, and therefore will run at 25fps if the mains frequency is truly 50Hz. Let us assume for the moment that the mains is at the right frequency and that when the tape recording was made the camera was running at exactly 25fps. The only variable that exists is the difference in speed between the tape recorders used for recording and replaying. If the replay tape recorder is running at exactly the same speed as the one used for recording then the frequency of the pilot tone on playback will be 50Hz. If not, then the pilot tone replay frequency is going to be different. In the second system for synchronous replay of pilot tone tapes, the frequency of the pilot tone on the tape is compared with that of the mains power supply, and the speed of the tape is adjusted so that both are equal. The comparison is done automatically by a device called a re-solver, now reduced in size to a printed circuit card which can be fitted inside the tape recorder. There is usually plus or minus 2.5% correction available to the speed of the tape, which can be increased by the addition of speed correctors which change the overall speed of the tape recorder. At no time does the transfer technician actually hear the pilot tone. The device which is resolving the synchronisation usually has some kind of display indicating the relationship between pilot tone and the external reference frequency. This is usually in the form of a small oscilloscope screen or a meter.

When an oscilloscope is used, it is connected up in such a way that the sine wave from the external reference makes the dot move horizontally and the pilot tone from the tape makes the dot move vertically. If both tones are at the same frequency, the resultant pattern on the screen will be circular (a Lissajous figure).

When a meter is used it is usually the kind in which the needle lies in the centre of the scale when it is not functioning (a centre zero meter). If there is no difference in the frequency of the pilot tone from the tape and the external reference, the needle will remain in the centre of the scale. When there is a difference between the frequency of the pilot tone from the tape and the external reference the resolver starts to operate, changing the speed of the tape so that both frequencies are the same. The shape of the circle on the oscilloscope squashes horizontally or vertically, and the needle of the meter moves to the left or right, depending on whether the speed of the recorder has been increased or decreased. At plus or minus 2.5% of difference in the two frequencies the resolver will cease to function properly and synchronisation will be lost. When this happens the circle on the oscilloscope starts to flop over itself and the needle on the meter sways backwards and forwards across the scale.

It is important for the sound recordist to make sure that the people who make the transfer know what the ratio is between the camera speed and the frequency of pilot tone.

All reference so far has been to pilot tone. There are other systems in use which are just as effective. They vary mostly in the way in which the synchronising signal is applied to the tape. The system in commonest use in the film industry is Neo-Pilot Tone as devised by Stephan Kudelski, the designer of the Nagra tape recorders.

Push-Pull Neo-Pilot Tone Recording

The signal from the camera is recorded on two narrow strips down the centre

Close-up of neo-pilot tone head showing location of pilot tone tracks.

of the tape. No attempt is made to separate these tracks from the main audio recording made across the whole width of the tape. However, although the pilot tone recording is superimposed over the audio it is not replayed because the two tracks are recorded 180° out of phase. Thus the head used for the pilot tone is called a push-pull head. The effect when playing back the audio is that only the audio is replayed because the pilot tone signal cancels itself out. When playing back the pilot tone signal on the push pull head, only the pilot comes through since the audio signal has the effect of being out of phase for that head.

Other Systems Using Pilot Tone From the Camera

(1) *Perfectone:* Push pull tracks are recorded along the edge of the tape, the audio being recorded between the synchronising tracks. When replayed on a full-track tape recorder there is no sync tone breakthrough. Sometimes this system uses 100Hz or 120Hz, in other words double the mains frequency.

(2) *Ranger Tone:* A head at an acute angle to the standard azimuth records a 14KHz tone down the centre of the tape. This is so far from the correct azimuth that it cannot be heard by the replay head. This tone is modulated with the pilot tone from the camera, and demodulated during replay.

(3) *Synchrotone:* Used when stereo synchronous recordings are made. Synchrotone is a separate third track down the centre of the two stereo tracks. It is not push-pull. In the Nagra version of this, a 13.5KHz signal is recorded and modulated with the sync information. It is also possible to record slating information on this track.

Other Considerations Relating to Pilot Tone Recording

The smallest professional tape recorder available at the moment is the Nagra SN. This uses narrow 1/8th inch (3.175mm) tape which leaves no space for recording a pair of push-pull tracks. Therefore the sync signal has to be recorded with the audio. In order to make sure that there is no interference between the two signals the frequency of the sync signal has been reduced to 10Hz. Simple filters separate the two on replay. There is an added advantage because the frequency chosen can be related to both 50- and 60Hz by division when filming and by multiplication during replay. There is a suggestion that on tape recorders using a push-pull pilot recording or synchrotone that the frequency of 600Hz may be more appropriate than 50- or 60Hz for the same reason. This would give the added advantage that should it be necessary to edit a tape containing a synchronising signal there will be less likelihood of a jump in the signal at the cut.

Synchro-Pulse

The early system already referred to known as Leevers-Rich Synchro-Pulse has virtually been replaced by pilot tone. It is still used, in fact has seen an upsurge in use in the amateur world for synchronising 8mm cameras with cassette recorders.

In the camera there is a pair of contacts which close every time a frame of film goes through the gate. A connecting cable transmits this to the tape recorder where a tone oscillator is activated. Thus, on a separate track of the tape, a series of pulses is recorded, one for each time the camera exposes a frame of film. All it is necessary to do is to make sure that there is a pulse replayed every time a frame of film goes through the magnetic film recorder. Therefore the film

S ⟶ N = MAGNETIC FIELD.

PILOT TONE HEAD
READS SYNC SIGNAL
ONLY SINCE THE TWO
HEADS IN TANDEM ARE
CONNECTED TOGETHER
OUT OF PHASE.

AUDIO REPLAY HEAD
READS AUDIO ONLY
SINCE PILOT TONE
TRACKS ARE OUT OF
PHASE AND THUS
CANCEL EACH OTHER
OUT.

PILOT TONE
OUTPUT

REPLAY
AMP

The pilot tone amplifier
is wired up in such a
way that the audio sig-
nal which has been re-
corded across the whole
of the tape will cancel
itself out but the pilot
tone tracks, which are
recorded out of phase,
will reinforce them-
selves, since for this amplifier they will be in
phase, thus ensuring
separation between au-
dio and pilot tone.

↑ = DIRECTION OF
SIGNAL FROM
AUDIO

↥ = DIRECTION OF
SIGNAL FROM
PILOT TONE

A

B

NEO-PILOT TONE

PERFECTONE

RANGERTONE

SYNCHROTONE

Track positions for various synchronising systems.

recorder is fitted with a similar set of contacts. They trigger the horizontal movement of the moving dot in an oscilloscope. The pulses on the tape are fed into the vertical amplifier of the 'scope to make the pulse visible. When the pulse remains stationary on the trace the tape recorder is running at the correct speed. The adjustment is manual, and only a short amount of practice is needed before it becomes easy to hold sync accurately. In the 8mm systems the process becomes more and more automatic and seems to work very well. There are many variations.

Pilot Tone Connections Between the Camera and the Tape Recorder

Pilot tone works very well. Literally hundreds of thousands of feet of film are shot every day using pilot tone for synchronisation. The weakest link in the system is the cable which links the camera to the tape recorder. The maintenance of this link seems to be the responsibility of the sound recordist. The diagram (on page 108) shows how the cable should be connected for pilot tone and silent turnover (which will be dealt with in the next section). It will be noticed that there is also a diagram for the use of cannon plugs at the camera end. This is because some users have rightly considered the DIN standard plug to be too delicate for the job. Since it is a three-pin cannon plug that has to be used some people use a microphone cable for the pilot tone cable. It is a simple matter to make a short adaptor lead for plugging into the tape recorder. Another adaptor cable can be used if the camera only has the DIN standard plug. The obvious advantage of this is that there is no need for carrying an extra lead. On the other hand if there is going to be a lot of hand-held camera work it is an advantage to use a curly telephone receiver cable for the pilot lead. This allows a certain amount of freedom yet does not get tangled in one's feet.

Whatever happens, it is always a good idea to have a spare pilot tone cable at hand. These cables are handled by both the sound and camera crews, they get

Top: *The Nagra SN.* Below: *Frequency response curves for Nagra SN.*

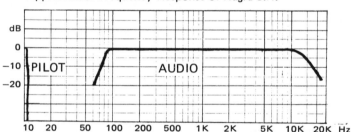

trod upon, and are generally subjected to greater strain than microphone cables, and are therefore more likely to give trouble. They are sometimes called *pulse* cables, a hangover from the days when synchro-pulse was used.

Silent Turn Over

With the advent of the portable tape recorder and the lightweight self-blimped camera, the camera and sound crews have been liberated. The transistor has been a major factor in reducing the size of equipment. Now crews can go almost everywhere in the world. The technicians who stay at home keep on improving the equipment and adding new ideas when they turn up. Those working in the field sometimes provide these ideas. Stephan Kudelski says that he designs the equipment and then waits to see what new things the people who use the equipment will do with it.

One of the first things to happen was the silent clapper board. News and *cinéma verité* crews realised that the presence of the clapper board betrayed when

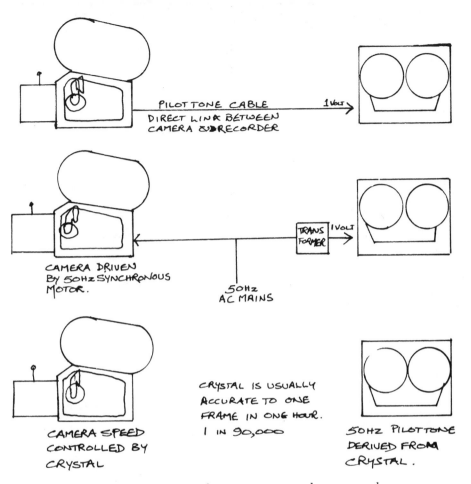

Pilot tone connections between camera and tape recorder.

the camera was running. This had an adverse effect on the people in front of the camera. So, cameras were designed with a small light built into the gate which would fog the film during the time taken for the mechanism to run up to speed. At the same time a signal was sent to the tape recorder on a separate wire, switching on a small oscillator in the recorder in order to record tone on the tape. The last frame of the tone could be matched with the last fogged frame on the picture in order to establish synchronisation. This removed the need for the clapper on a clapper board but did not provide any other information. Further systems relating to automatic scene marking will be dealt with later.

Crystal Sync

For the *cinéma verité* crew the most annoying piece of equipment is the pilot tone cable. Pilot tone establishes the speed of the camera on the tape, a relationship which can be re-established during transfer. Crystal synchronisation ensures

EARTH

PILOT

"CLAPPER"

NAGRA 3
(MALE PLUG)

DIN STANDARD
PLUG (FEMALE) ON
ARRIFLEX 16BL

"CLAPPER"

PILOT

EARTH

NAGRA 4.
PIN 3 IS PILOT
OUTPUT FROM
BUILT-IN CRYSTAL
(FEMALE PLUG)

LINKING PINS 4 & 5
ON CAMERA PLUG
INITIATES SILENT TURNOVER
"CLAPPER"

"CLAPPER" IS POSITIVE WITH RESPECT TO EARTH

Above: *The correct connections for a pilot tone lead between an Arriflex camera and Nagra.* Below: *Pilot tone lead in use.*

that the camera is running at a true 24- or 25fps. An oscillator of extreme accuracy can be constructed by incorporating a crystal in the circuit. By comparing the frequency of this oscillator with a reference frequency from the camera mechanism it is possible to control the speed of the camera to an accuracy of one part in fifty thousand. A similar crystal oscillator in the tape recorder provides the pilot tone which is recorded on the tape. Since we know that the camera is running at the right speed, and an alarm in the camera indicates if this is not true, the pilot tone on the tape now indicates the speed of the tape at the time of recording. The effect is the same as using a pilot tone lead, and is accurate to one frame in half-an-hour of filming.

The design of camera crystal-controlled motors varies. On the Eclair NPR there is a switch which selects 24- or 25fps and the frequency of the pilot tone output which is available in case there is no crystal generator in the recorder. It is possible to fit a crystal oscillator inside the Nagra IV. On the older Nagra III however the oscillator has to be an external affair. An extremely small oscillator recently released by a London firm, Tycho Films, takes its power from the recorder and provides 50- or 60Hz switchable internally. It has an interesting extra facility. When the device is set for 50Hz it is possible to switch on a small light emitting diode which glows at a rate of 25 flashes per second. By pointing the camera at the LED and looking through the viewfinder it is possible by checking for strobing to ascertain whether the camera is running at 25fps. This of course does not work for 24fps or 60Hz. It is useful to know too that if there is doubt about the speed of the camera it can be checked by pointing it at a 50Hz television screen. This again only works for 25fps but is accurate since the frame rate of television pictures is controlled very accurately by a crystal at the transmitter. In such cameras as Arriflex BL there is a black patch on the reflecting surface of the mirror shutter (which since it increases the number of flickers per second in the viewfinder, subjectively reduces flicker). This effectively blots out a few lines on the television image when viewed through the viewfinder of a running camera, creating a black bar across the picture. If this black bar moves up or down, there is a difference in speed between the camera and the television picture, and the camera is therefore not running at 25fps. If the effect is not visible in the viewfinder, it is well to examine the shutter to make sure that it has the flicker blade.

Radio Slating

The silent turnover facility on some cameras is only a synchronising mark on the sound and the film. It is not sufficient for an editor faced with many shots on many rolls of film. There is no real substitute for the clapper board since when it is used both the picture and the sound track are well documented with information about the shot. There are two elaborations of the silent clapper board which are worth examining.

The first made by Kudelski is for use with the Nagra and the Eclair camera fitted with crystal sync. The light behind the gate fogs the film in a specific sequence which can be adjusted at the camera. At the same time as fogging is taking place a signal is sent by wireless to the tape recorder and the pilot tone signal being applied to the tape is interrupted.

The radio slating device is triggered by the silent clapper in the camera and at the same time sends a radio signal which interrupts the pilot on the recorder. There can be no confusion in the recorder that a radio signal from the camera

•*A Tycho CN3 Crystal for use with the Nagra III. This is fitted with a light emitting diode for checking the speed of the camera (arrowed). This does not work when the crystal is set for 60Hz operation.*

is present since two signals are sent at the same time and if both are not present the recorder's receiver does not react. After the signal put on by the camera the Kudelski system takes over and fogs the film three more times, two frames at a time. The space left between each pulse indicates the number selected at the camera. Thus if 999 is the number selected there will be 18 frames (or double the number) left between each pulse. The spacing between pulses is worked out by a timing circuit and is accurate for 25fps. If necessary the slating can be set to take place at the end of a shot thus making it possible for the camera operator to start a shot and be sure that it can be used right from the beginning. This is alright providing the film does not run out before the end of the shot. The three numbers provided do not need to be used as a sequential numbering system from zero. They could be divided as follows:

No. 1: Camera number
No. 2: Roll number
No. 3: Shot number on the roll.

Thus it will be seen that many cameras can be used on one sequence, say a pop concert, with the tape recorder running all the time. The radio pulses from the camera do not interfere with the audio signal being recorded since they are recorded by omission of pilot tone. The use of many cameras is possible without confusion provided they don't all start at the same time.

In transfer it is possible to get tone put on the film whenever there is no pilot tone. This transfer can be used to provide the editor with sound

A Tycho CN4 crystal circuit board inside a Nagra IV. The arrow shows the light emitting diode which can be used for checking the speed of the camera at 25fps.

Television screens can be used in 50Hz countries to check the speed of the camera. If the bar that is visible across the screen when viewed through the viewfinder of a running camera remains stationary the speed is 25fps.

information for synchronisation purposes. After synchronisation this film transfer will no longer be needed and has to be replaced with one which does not have the pips (alternatively it is possible to transfer the pips to a separate track on the film, removing the need for a second transfer). There is one problem. Since the pilot tone head is between the record head and the replay head the relationship of the pilot tone to audio signal is reversed. The result is that the pips transferred to the film are out of sync by about 5 frames (when the tape has been recorded at 7.5ips). Provided that the editor knows this there is little problem.

There are three radio frequencies available. These have to be sorted out by mutual agreement when more than one film unit is shooting the same event if unbelievable confusion is to be avoided

The second system, called *crystamatic,* is made by Audio Engineering Limited in London. It provides crystal control for the motor in an Arriflex BL as well as radio slating. For the numbering of the takes the system relies on the probability that the camera operator will not need to take more than ten shots in a 400ft (122m) roll of 16mm film. Every time the camera button is pressed the counter registers another shot. At the start of the shot there is a long flash which lasts until the camera speed has stabilised, and then a series of short flashes, the number of flashes coinciding with the number of the shot. These flashes are repeated at the end of the take when the camera is switched off, the camera continuing to run automatically until the marking is finished. At the flick of a switch it is possible to have the marking take place at the end of the shot only. Every time there is a flash a tone is transmitted to the tape recorder

112

Above: *Crystamatic Radio Slating apparatus fitted to an Arriflex BL.*

Photo: *Audio Engineering Ltd.*

Below: *One method of using the Crystamatic.*

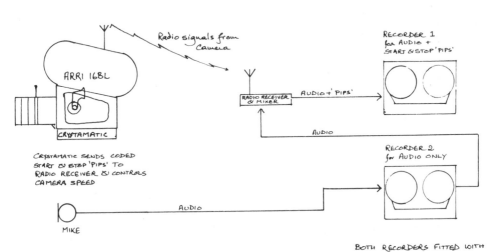

and recorded on the tape. The radio link can be used while the camera is not running for the camera operator to talk to the sound recordist. Three frequencies are allocated in Great Britain for radio slating, 161MHz, 161.05MHz, and 161.075MHz and these are available at a channel selector to enable three units to work in the same area at the same time without interference. The differentiation between each camera is made by adjusting the pitch of the audio signal recorded on the tape.

At the tape recorder end of the link there is a receiver that records the camera operator's remarks and the pips. There is, therefore no difference in sync between the pips and the audio. In a single camera operation the resultant recording can provide the editor with a lot of useful information, but when a multi-camera set-up is being used to film a continuous performance such as a conference or pop concert the pips and camera operator's remarks become a nuisance. This information has therefore to be kept separate by recording it on a second recorder or on the second track of a two-track machine.

Summary of Synchronising Systems

Single-system uses the same piece of film to record both the picture and the sound. Since there is a separation between the sound and the picture it is difficult to edit while both remain on the same piece of film. This disadvantage is compensated for by the reduction of equipment while shooting, and the certainty of synchronisation. Used extensively for news in television.

Double-system is more versatile than single-system and is the most common. It is broken into two separate classes, film and tape. Double-system using film for the sound is not very common any more because of the weight of the film recorder. Using tape and a synchronising signal is more common. This can again be broken into two categories, pilot tone with a sync lead, and crystal sync. With the lead the pilot tone establishes the exact ratio between the speed of the camera and the tape, a relationship which can be re-established during transfer of the tape to film. With crystal sync the speed of the camera is exactly governed and the pilot tone recorded on the tape from a crystal oscillator of similar accuracy is a guide to the speed of the tape during recording. Crystal sync replaces the sync lead.

The important thing to remember about pilot tone is that the operator making the transfer to film must be informed of the ratio of camera speed to pilot tone frequency.

Other Uses of Pilot Tone

In the filming of musicals it is important to record all the music before the shooting of the film. This is far more convenient than trying to shoot the sound shot by shot. The difficulties of matching the takes for sound quality and musicianship is far too great. In shooting musicals the sound is played back to the actors and they mime the action and singing in time to the music. The process is useless unless the sound is played back in sync every time. The tape carrying the music has to be recorded with pilot tone. In playback the speed of the tape is regulated by pilot tone from a camera or from a crystal if the camera has a crystal motor by comparison of the pilot tone signals in a sync resolver. Another tape recorder is used to record the music and the clapper board as an indication of sync for the editor (known as a guide track). As in radio slating this recording will be discarded when the film has been edited.

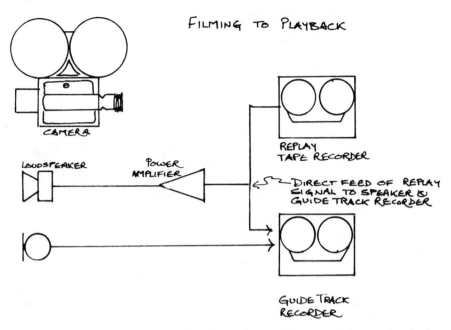

CAMERA

LOUDSPEAKER

POWER AMPLIFIER

REPLAY TAPE RECORDER

DIRECT FEED OF REPLAY SIGNAL TO SPEAKER & GUIDE TRACK RECORDER

GUIDE TRACK RECORDER

Camera, replay tape recorder and guide track recorder must all be synchronised to the same reference signal. This could be: (a) Pilot tone generator on the camera, (b) common mains driving both camera and pilot tone on the recorders, (c) crystal generators for the camera and both recorders. (N.B. In systems (b) and (c) it is possible to use more than one camera.)

Multi-Camera Set-Ups

When more than one camera is used it is not necessary to have a separate tape recorder for each camera (as has already been indicated in the section on radio slating). The important thing is that the cameras must all run at the same speed and the pilot tone must come from a similar source to that driving the cameras. Crystal sync has already been discussed. Since all the cameras are being driven at the correct speed they must all be running at the same speed. Provided the pilot tone is also recorded from a matching crystal, synchronisation will be achieved.

It is also possible to use the mains to drive the cameras. If all the cameras are driven by synchronous motors powered from the same mains source they will all run at the same speed. The tape recorder must therefore get its pilot tone signal from the mains. A transformer must be used to reduce the voltage to about 1 volt. *Never feed more than 1½ volts into the pilot tone input of a tape recorder.* If in doubt check the voltage with a meter, since to feed more than 1½ volts into a Nagra III for instance, does considerable damage which will make the recorder inoperable. In this case if the frequency of the mains varies, as it will, the speed of the cameras will vary in proportion, as will the frequency of the pilot tone being recorded on the tape. Thus the ratio remains constant and the tape can be transferred in sync at a later stage.

Nagra III with an ATN attached. The ATN provides DC for the recorder as well as 1½ volts AC for feeding pilot tone to the recorder from the mains. The pilot tone socket on the recorder is the lower one.

Because the mains frequency is not stable (the variation is small), crystal sync cannot be mixed with mains sync.

If radio slating is being used there is no need to worry if all the cameras are started at different times. If not, then in a multi-camera set-up it will be necessary to start all the cameras at the same time and mark the beginning of the take with a clapperboard. It is obvious that in a multi-camera set-up it would be stupid to start marking the shots in the middle of the sound take with a clapper board.

Some people use a crystal driven clock to provide synchronising information in multi-camera set-ups. When the clock is started a 'pip' is recorded on the tape (on which pilot tone from a crystal oscillator is being recorded.) At the start of each shot all that the camera operators need do is point their cameras at the clock. When the editor is synchronising the rushes he uses the 'pip' on the sound track as a start mark for a time counter on his editing machine. Thus, to synchronise picture with sound all he has to do is look at the clock in the picture and match it with the appropriate sound track.

Chapter V

Transfer from Tape to Film

As has been said before, the most practical way to work with a sound track when editing a film is to have that sound track recorded on film. It is also important to have the master sound track transferred in case anything should happen to the film during editing. This should be done even if the original sound track is mastered directly on film.

The company which does the transfer must get certain information if they are going to be able to perform the task of transfer correctly:

(1) The size of the film to transfer to—35mm or 16mm.
(2) The speed of the transfer—24fps or 25fps.
(3) In 16mm—centre track or edge track.
(4) The type or format of the sync. signal on the tape.
(5) The ratio between the camera speed and the pilot tone frequency.
(6) The level at which the transfer should be made.

They should also be informed of the title of the film, the tape roll number and information about the shots. In some cases they should know where to deliver the rushes.

The sound recordist is responsible for keeping the sound report sheet containing most of this information. There are several different types of sheet and some examples are printed on adjoining pages. It will be noticed that although the layout is different the information contained is much the same. The number of copies needed varies from company to company. Some recordists just write the information on the tape box and the transfer technician transfers the information to a sound report which accompanies the film to the editor. It is important that the editor gets this sheet since it may contain information about the quality of the recording.

At the beginning of the roll the sound recordist should record the following information (if there is time):

(1) The production company and number.
(2) The title of the film.
(3) The tape roll number.
(4) The date.
(5) The place of recording.
(6) The tape speed and the recorder number.
(7) The camera speed and the size of film to transfer to.
(8) The type of pilot tone and the frequency.
(9) The type of slating—if radio slating.
(10) The level of reference tone.
(11) A reference tone.

A cunning sound recordist will record this information on the beginning of several rolls of tape at the start of day so that not too much time is taken in changing rolls of tape.

The reference tone referred to in (11) above can only be recorded if the

SOUND REPORT

Production	The Documentary	DD620	Date 24-1-77

Tape roll № TWELVE	7·5 ips	16 mm

Sync system XTAL ✦	50 Hz	25 fps

Slate	Take	Length	Remarks —8dB Tone
47	1	26	Aeroplane
	2	29	
	3	30	Slight camera noise
	④	24	
48	①	14	BOARD ON END
	②	15	BOE
49	1	12	⎱
	2	11	⎰ Bad camera noise
	③	13	⎱
WT49x	1		Wild track —covers slate 49.
FX17	1		BUZZ TRACK —PUB
50	1		BAD TRAFFIC BG.
	2		
	3		Acceptable quality on dialogue
FX18	1		Filling beer mug from tap.
FX19	1		"LAST ORDERS PLEASE"
51	1		Sync
	2		Camera run out.
	3		
	4		

A sound report issued with a transfer from ¼ inch tape to 16mm film.

studiosound

Nº 5069 **A**

mercury group of companies

86 wardour street london W1 telephone 01-734 0263/4

WESTREX   RCA   DOLBY SYSTEM

CUSTOMER: Documentary films	ORDER No: 90631	DATE: 27th Aug 76
	PROD. No: 49	CHANNEL: 16mm RCA
	TITLE: BUILDING	

SLATE No.	DESCRIPTION	TAKE	FOOTAGE	LENGTH	REMARKS
99		1	0	43	Board on End
		2		84	BoE
100		1		99	
		2		115	
		3		132	
101		1		160	BoE
Fx 49		1		190	
102		1		210	
		3		230	
		6		252	
Fx 50		2		275	
WT 103X		1		280	
		2		285	
		3		291	

FROM	¼"	(PULSE)	(MONO)	35 m MAG	16 m MAG	35 m OPT	CASSETTE		DOLBY	A
	SPEED 7·5 ips	STEREO	TK	EDGE	CENTRE	16 m OPT	MONO	STEREO		B
TO	¼"	PULSE	MONO	35 m MAG	(16 m MAG)	35 m OPT	CASSETTE		DOLBY	A
	SPEED 24 fps	STEREO	TK	EDGE	(CENTRE)	16 m OPT	MONO	STEREO		B

Signature _____

A sound report sheet as made out by the sound recordist on location. Details of the gauge of the film and the speed of the transfer are important. Other remarks made in the remarks column can help the editor decide whether to use the sound on that shot or not.

119

facility exists on the tape recorder. It is very important to record this tone if the transfer level is to remain consistent from tape roll to tape roll and from day to day.

There are two common standards for reference tone:

(1) Tone recorded at 100% modulation, i.e., at 0dB on the meter.

(2) Tone recorded at zero level or —8dB on the meter.

It doesn't matter which standard is used provided that the transfer technician knows which it is. To be absolutely certain it is a good idea to actually state the reading of the needle on the scale of the meter.

The slating at the beginning of a roll of tape may read something like this, "Commercial films production commercial number XYZ/30/41, roll number 2, 20th December 1973, shooting in the studio. Nagra three number 5055 at 7.5ips. Crystal pilot tone at 50Hz. Transfer to 35mm at 24fps. —8dB tone for transfer."

As will be noticed most of this information is duplicated in the sheet which accompanies the tape.

Philosophies of Transfer

There are two schools of thought on transfer.

(1) All transfers should be listened to and evaluated. If necessary the transfer should be filtered in order to provide the dubbing mixer with a clean track.

(2) All transfers should be made without equalisation and at a standard level, leaving the dubbing mixer to make the manipulations as he sees fit.

I personally prefer the second school of thought. The dubbing mixer has more control. Since it is he who sees the final film for the first time, the sound from different shots juxtaposed for the first time, it is surely he who should make the judgement about levels and filtering. The transfer technician does not have this advantage. Besides which, he is usually transferring so much diverse material from many different sources that he cannot possibly remember from day to day the equalisation settings that he has chosen for one particular production. The situation also arises that the editor wants to get a shot or two retransferred, a process which is useless unless the quality of transfer is consistent.

Reference Tone

The reference tone is important because it tells the transfer technician what the recording level of the recorder is. If he knows what level the reference tone was recorded at he will set the volume control on the film recorder so that the needle on the meter goes to the same point. This will usually mean that he has only to make a minor adjustment to the normal setting of the machine because there is very little difference in the recording level of different tape recorders. If there is a difference which is notable the procedure is simple. The replay channel is checked by replaying a recording of known value, i.e. a test tape. If the equipment checks out then the value of noting down the number of the tape recorder used becomes apparent. The sound recordist can be told to have his equipment tested.

Equipment Normally Found in a Transfer Suite

The minimum equipment needed for transfer is as follows:

(1) 35mm recorder

(2) 16mm recorder

(3) A sync replay tape recorder e.g. Nagra III or IV
(4) Bulk tape and film eraser
(5) Oscillator
(6) Oscilloscope and good AC voltmeter
(7) Test tapes and films

In this list there are only three vital pieces of audio equipment. While the list remains simple the time is right to introduce the concept of the *patch panel.*

We will assume that the equipment is permanently mounted and cannot be easily moved.

A patch panel is a board on which are mounted a series of rows of telephone jack-plug sockets. The audio connections to and from each piece of equipment are soldered to the terminals of each socket. Thus we may find that the patch panel is marked up as follows:

35mm Recorder IN	16mm Recorder IN	NAGRA IN	CASSETTE IN	MONITOR IN	TIE LINES TO MAIN STUDIO 1	2	3
O	O	O	O	O	O	O	O

35mm Recorder OUT	16mm Recorder OUT	NAGRA OUT	CASSETTE IN	35mm REPLAY OUT	16mm REPLAY OUT	DISC OUT	
O	O	O	O	O	O	O	O

SIMPLE TRANSFER BAY PATCH PANEL

In this way all the connections for audio in the transfer suite are brought to the same point. The connections that need to be made between any item are made using leads with jack plugs at each and called patch cords. For example if it is necessary to make a transfer from tape to 35mm film the connection would be made from *tape out* to *35 in.* This would make the transfer possible but the technician would not be able to hear the results unless he made a connection between *35 out* and *Mon in* (standing for monitor amplifier input). A switch on the film recorder would enable him to check the difference between the input and replay signals, the A-B test. The oscillator output is there so that tone is easily available for setting bias on the recorder. It will be necessary to mention patch panels again when the subject of dubbing theatres comes up. There is nothing to fear about them provided they are properly marked up and logically laid out. They are easy to work provided that a cool mind is kept and the steps required in order to make a connection are thought out first.

The other pieces of equipment mentioned in the list, the oscilloscope, AC volt meter, and the test tapes and films, are vital for maintaining the transfer equipment at peak performance. The bulk tape- and film-eraser can be used for cleaning stock that is to be re-used. In most cases new stock is always used for transfers, but provided that second-hand stock is checked and bulk-erased there is no reason why it should not be re-used for 35mm transfers. Second-hand 16mm stock is always suspect and should be very carefully checked. The use of second-hand stock does not effect much saving and as already indicated could be a false economy.

Other equipment which is useful in a transfer suite is a turntable, cassette recorder, and a replay tape machine which has facilities for half- and quarter-track and the very low speeds like 3.75ips (9.525cm/s) and 1.875ips (4.7625cm/s).

Patch panel in a transfer suite.

The magnetic film recorders should be equipped with gears for both 24- and 25fps. If they are driven by synchronous motors it will be possible for transfers to be made in sync from 35mm to 16mm and vice versa. One of the machines should be equipped with a shaft-driven 60Hz alternator, i.e. 60Hz when running at 24fps. This enables transfers to be made from tapes which have been recorded using 60Hz pilot tone. Of course in the USA and other 60Hz countries it would be useful to have a 50Hz shaft-driven alternator, but it must be able to work at both 24- and 25fps. It is only necessary to have one machine fitted with the alternator since (a) there will be few transfers of this nature to do, and (b) if the transfer has to be done to the other gauge then both machines can be run in order to provide the reference pilot signal, and since they are both driven by synchronous motors they will both be running at the same speed and the frequency will therefore be correct.

I point this out because I have had occasion to record tracks for American units who have wanted transfer in Britain, and have yet wanted the pilot signal on the tape to conform with their own standards in order to avoid complications at their end.

The Transfer Process

(It will be noticed that this book has so far avoided discussion on the techniques of sound recording. This is because I feel that the sound recording process cannot be viewed in a vacuum. The reader should get an idea of the processes involved before approaching the task of recording a sound.)

The transfer technician will get a roll of tape and a sound report. From the sheet he will know what to transfer since the takes to be transferred will be

122

circled. For this reason it is vital that the sound recordist logs every sound that is recorded on the tape. It is important to slate (identify) every take too.

The procedure for transfer is as follows.

Raw film is placed on the film recorder and the bias set. This will take about 15 feet (4.6m) in 16mm and 30 feet (9m) in 35mm. If economy is the order of the day a loop of film can be used for this biasing process.

The replay tape recorder is patched to the film recorder.

Synchronisation details are checked from the sheet and the speed of the film recorder adjusted.

The volume control on the recorder is adjusted so that the meter reads the same as specified for the reference tone.

The tape is then run through to the first take to be transferred. If this is the first take on the tape then it is not a bad idea to listen to a bit of it to make sure that the sound quality is alright and that the synchronisation is taking place as one would expect.

The tape must then be rewound to the start of the take.

The film recorder is run up to speed and switched to record. This could take up to five seconds worth of film.

The replay machine is then started and the film recorder switched to replay so that the quality of the recording on the film can be monitored constantly.

If the next take to be transferred follows on immediately the film recorder is left running. If not it is stopped and only restarted when the next take to be transferred is found. (It will be noticed that there is considerable wastage of film stock every time the film recorder is stopped and started. The knowledge that editors realise this is sometimes the excuse for adding a percentage onto the length of the transferred footage. Transfer suites survive on this hidden profit, and it is only spot checks on the length of transferred footage next to the invoice that will eradicate the practice.)

Economy is the order of the day for some small documentary film units. Transfers can be made more economically if some time is used in cutting out the undesirable takes in a tape. In this way it is possible for the transfer to go through without stops and starts thus avoiding the wastage. This is not a professional practice and may be more expensive in the time consumed by the editing. Tape is very delicate and the extra handling may do irreparable damage.

The transfer will be sent to the editor with a report which may well comment on the quality of some of the takes. If the transfer is made at a transfer suite which is a department of a dubbing theatre it is well to take note of these comments.

In the final stages of the production of a sound track for a film the track is transferred to optical sound film. This is a specialised form of transfer which will be dealt with in a later chapter.

Chapter VI

Editing Sound

This chapter is basically aimed at the person who is going to need to edit sound tracks. In the film unit there are two people who are involved in sound editing. The editor is the person who sees to the completion of the picture during the editing stage and therefore inevitably comes into contact with the sound track. The dubbing editor prepares the film for the final mixing process. It is important for the sound recordist to know about both these processes since they vitally affect the way in which a track is recorded and the material which is gathered.

Sound editing can completely change the meaning of a sentence. When well done the results are indistinguishable from an original recording. Music can be lengthened, shortened, assembled from many tapes. Sound effects can obtain new meaning from editing. Bad sound editing is immediately discernible to the trained ear and discomforting to the average listener.

Firstly, sound editing on 1/4 inch (6.25mm) tape.

Equipment Needed for Editing Tape

What is needed is a splicing block, a sharp razor blade, a spirit-based felt-tipped marker, and a roll of 1/4 inch (6.25mm) joining tape. The tape recorder on which the editing is to be done must be one on which it is possible to wind the tape by hand with the tape in contact with the replay head. This means that the editor will be able to wind the tape slowly past the head, enabling him to hear exactly the point where he wants to cut.

Equipment needed for editing 1/4 inch tape.

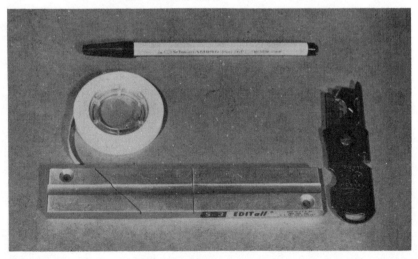

Above: *A Leevers-Rich studio tape recorder showing the splicing block, and most important of all, the easy access to the heads which makes the machine very easy to edit on.*

SPLICING BLOCK

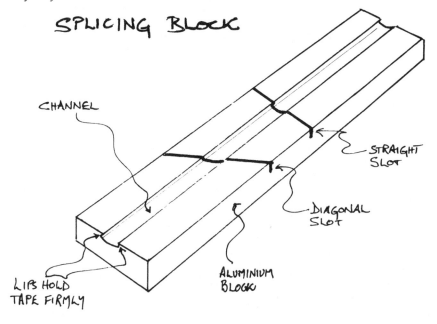

CHANNEL

STRAIGHT SLOT

DIAGONAL SLOT

ALUMINIUM BLOCK

LIPS HOLD TAPE FIRMLY

125

Using the Joining or Splicing Block

We will examine the methods for finding the point at which the tape is to be cut in the next sections, but must for the moment assume that those points have been found and marked. Reference to the diagram will show the parts of the joining block referred to in this section. The block has a channel along its length. The overlapping edges hold the tape in place. Two narrow slots across the groove, one diagonal and one at right angles, enable a razor blade to be accurately guided when cutting the tape. The diagonal cut is best for most purposes because it makes a join which crosses the head progressively in what is effectively a very quick dissolve from one sound to another. A straight cut can sometimes make a noise on replay.

Press the tape emulsion down into the channel so that the edges hold it. Then slide the tape along the channel so that the mark is over the diagonal slot. Line up the razor blade in the slot and cut the tape, using a slicing movement. Never saw at the tape since this leaves ragged edges, and has the further effect of blunting the blade when it comes into contact with the bottom of the slot. Only the tip of the blade should touch the bottom of the slot. Remove the unwanted piece of tape and repeat the procedure for the other piece of tape. Slide the cut pieces of tape along the channel so that the place where the sticky tape is going to be applied does not lie over a slot. Making the join in such a place can distort the tape slightly. Cut off about one inch (25.4mm) of joining tape, accurately align it parallel to the edges of the channel, and press it gently onto the tape where the two ends butt together. It is better to use vertical pressure when making the join than a stroking pressure. This latter can cause the joining tape to stretch which creates a tension liable to make the tape curl at the join. Clean hands are essential when handling the sticky tape if its adhesive qualities are not to be lost. In practice it does not seem to matter much if a slight amount of sticky tape can be seen from the emulsion side of the tape, but the ideal is an absolute butt join without any overlap. It is possible to damage the edges of the joined tape when removing it from the groove in the joining block. To avoid this lift the tape at both ends of the block and then pull outwards so that the tape is flipped out of the groove. Do not on any account peel the tape out of the groove.

Patience and application for half-an-hour is usually enough for the user to become proficient at manipulating tape in a joining block.

Finding the Cutting Point—Speech

There are usually three reasons for wanting to cut sound.
(1) To get rid of unwanted material.
(2) To shorten the material.
(3) To change the meaning of the material.
There is virtually no point in editing sound if the cut is going to be obvious. There are two things which will make a cut obvious.
(1) If the rhythm and the sense of the sound is lost.
(2) If the background noise changes at the cut.
Speech has a definite rhythm, even if it is rather random (the rhythm in music is perhaps better defined and more regular). The sense implicit in speech is vital to understanding. The following two sentences may illustrate the point.

"I wanted to go to the shop in main street."

126

"So I took the number 16 bus and got off at Side Road."
For the sake of the example it may suit our purposes to cut the sentences together to make:

"I wanted to go to the shop in / Side Road."
It would not be much use if after cutting it sounded like:

"I wanted to go to the shop in/f at Side Road."
The rhythm of speech is usually defined by the times the speaker has to take a breath, which usually co-incides with the beginnings and ends of sentences. The tone of voice, speaking, whispering and shouting, may to a degree also define rhythm. The rhythm of speech is completely lost if the natural pauses for breathing and thinking are removed. In losing the rhythm some of the sense is lost and the speech becomes unreal. Rather like printing abookwithoutanyspacesbetweenthewords.

The easiest way to shorten dialogue is to remove whole sentences and paragraphs. There may be the need to remove sentence 'B' from a paragraph containing sentences 'A', 'B', and 'C'. The tape is run through the tape recorder until the pause between sentences 'A' and 'B' is found. Then find the beginning of sentence 'B', winding the tape past the head slowly by hand. Finding the actual spot involves winding the tape past the beginning of the sentence and

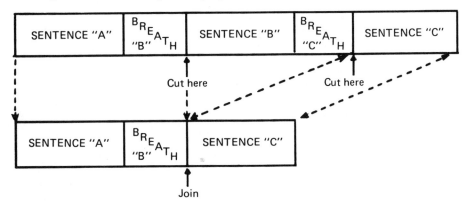

An almost infallible rule for joining speech, it is easy to find the start of a sound and leaving the breath in maintains a natural rhythm. The system breaks down when sentence "B" is an exclamation, people usually take a sharp breath before an exclamation and thus breath "B" may be unsuitable for sentence "C".

then winding back in a see-saw action until the exact point is found. It is quite difficult for the untutored ear. What is needed is a visual aid. Watch a point on the edge of the tape reel, even make a mark on the edge of the reel. Mark the tape at a point near the cutting point. Both these aids make it easier for the beginner to find the cutting point, especially when it comes to cutting music. It is important to move the tape briskly past the head. If it is moved too slowly the sound from the loudspeaker is too much of a mush with nothing coherent to he heard for accurate working. Once the beginning of sentence 'B' has been found the place to cut is marked. The procedure is repeated for the beginning of sentence 'C', and the two sentences 'A' and 'C' are joined together. It will be noticed that the intake of breath used for sentence 'B' is now being used for sentence 'C'. This is one of the few rules which works nearly every time for the cutting of speech. Always cut at the beginning of the sentence to be removed and use its breath to precede the new sentence. This would not work if sentence 'C' was an exclamation (usually preceded by a sharp intake of breath). There is another advantage in using this system. The background noise for sentence 'A' will continue behind the breath and any change will be camouflaged by the presence of the word at the beginning of sentence 'C'.

It is always easier to hear the beginning of a sound than the end. The ends of most sounds have echo attached and if this echo is cut into and as a result suddenly disappears the result is uncomfortable. Note also that the ends of words are difficult to find if the word ends with the letters B, D, F, G, P, and Z and especially the letters K, S, and T. For traps at the end of the word 'FACTS' is a good example. Close study will reveal spaces between FA and C and TS. Indeed there is sometimes no sound at all in these spaces.

Editing speech is very much a case of practice makes perfect. A skilful editor can manipulate single words and parts of words. This kind of feat needs a good sense of co-ordination between the hands, the eyes and the ears.

Finding the Cutting Point—Music

If a successful cut is to be made in a piece of music then there must be no sudden jarring of the musical rhythm, no loss of or sudden change in the tune, and no sudden illogical change in the musical key. I cannot pretend to be able to write about these factors, since I am no musician, nor am I versed in musical terminology. I can however say that music cutting is not difficult provided that the editor is absolutely honest about whether a join is alright or not. If there is the slightest doubt about the sense of the music after it has been cut then the cutting point is wrong, and it is pointless to kid oneself. It is harder to get away with a bad cut in music because there are such well defined conventions which music follows, and which almost everyone is familiar with.

If it is necessary to shorten a piece of music, then it is better to remove a whole 'verse' than to try to take out a bit here and there. This closely parallels the situation found in speech. It is necessary to listen to the music again and again, timing sections, and deciding whether they can be removed, before a decision can be taken about making a successful cut. When it has been decided which section can safely be removed then it becomes necessary to find a sharp sound in the music to cut on. The trouble with music is that there is frequently so much going on that the cutting point is difficult to hear. This becomes even more a problem when the music is wound through by hand. The type of note to look for should be percussive and well-defined. Having found the beginning of a section that can be removed then it is necessary to find the same point at the beginning of the next section. In other words, just as in cutting out a sentence in speech. If there is any doubt about the cut then leave in too much tape. This way it is possible to cut out small pieces and gradually make an adjustment; far better than having to add small sections. If the cut is to be made on a master tape, then be sure to practice on a copy first. Have a copy handy in case the master gets damaged.

The final test of any join is what it sounds like. If it is inaudible then the join is alright. The editor should not be fooled by his ear, and has to be honest.

Editing sound requires the type of concentration which some people call a 'good ear'.

Finding the Cutting Point—Effects

Cutting sound effects (FX) is generally easier than speech or music. Again practice and concentrated listening are essential. Having said that cutting FX is easier, I would just point out that selection and recording of FX which is often the job of the sound recordist can be extremely tricky (a subject which will be covered in a later chapter). There are three catagories into which FX can fall:

(1) Synchronous FX
(2) General FX (background atmosphere)
(3) Offscreen FX

Synchronous FX are best dealt with in conjunction with film sound editing (in a later section). There are two questions, however, which should be asked. If there are several FX which come from different sources, will they cut together without a noticeable change in background noise? Is the acoustic quality of the effect such that it will match with other FX and will it be possible to cut the end of the effect without cutting into any echo which may exist on the recording?

Again it is a question of listening, but it becomes necessary to listen in a qualitative way, often without having the advantage of seeing the film at the same time.

Background Atmospheres are sound FX which are added to a scene in order to establish a place and mood. They are not necessarily synchronous. Typical examples might be a supermarket, sea, wind, exhibition hall, audience noise, chatting people, traffic, waterfall, rain, refrigerator motor, office typewriters, generators and the interior of an aeroplane. There are countless different types of atmospheric sounds which can be recorded and which almost by definition are not suitable to the exact mood of the film. When used for film they will almost certainly be in the form of an endless loop (a long piece of film joined end to end). It is at this join that skill as a sound editor is sometimes needed.

The join in the loop must be inaudible so that with FX like traffic, wind, sea, which are variable in quality, the editor must find a point where the end and beginning of the loop match. Sometimes this is only done by trial and error.

Rhythmic sounds such as clocks ticking can also be presented as a loop. Joining the ends of the loop together in this case is much like editing music and care must be taken not to get a result like: "Tic toc, tic toc, tic toc toc, tic toc" etc.

Other non-synchronous background sound effects such as clocks striking produce special problems. A sound FX library will have various clock bells striking twelve. It may be important that the clock strike only three times. Logically one might take the first three rings. This is a mistake since the last one will not have the natural resonant dying away that is so characteristic of a bell. The correct strikes to use are the last three.

At the risk of being boring, I repeat that the sound editor has to learn how to listen. If there is no expert on hand to vet the results of editing sound then there has to be honesty built into the person doing the editing. Honesty and concentrated listening. It is no good saying "That's alright." The editor must be able to say "That's right."

Chapter VII

The Dubbing Theatre

The place known variously as: the dubbing theatre, re-recording studio, mixing studio, is where the final sound track for a film is made. It is basically divided into three parts: a machine room containing projectors and film sound equipment, a recording studio, and a theatre equipped with a mixing desk. Each of these rooms is sound-proofed so that there is no interference from the noises made by the equipment.

The main point of a dubbing theatre lies in its ability to run many pieces of equipment in exact synchronism. This means that the sound track for a film can be broken down into many separate components: dialogue, music and effects, and then mixed together in the desired proportions. The ability to run all the separate components in exact synchronism enables this process to take place easily. Recording sound in synchronism with the picture is also useful.

We will examine first the mechanical aspects of a dubbing theatre and then, in the next chapter, the ways in which the editor can get the best out of the equipment and technicians.

Synchronism

As mentioned in the chapter on transfer, the importance of using film (as opposed to tape) for film sound in the editing and dubbing process is that, since the sound film is perforated in the same way and with the same dimensions as the picture film, synchronisation between the two elements, picture and sound, is easily maintained. In the dubbing theatre it is necessary to run many film reproducers, a film recorder and a projector in synchronism with each other. But these separate machines must not only run at the same speed, but must also start and stop at the same rate. In other words if the film is exactly 800 feet long, and this means that each of its associated sound tracks will also be 800 feet long, then the synchronisation in a dubbing theatre means that if you start all the sound tracks and the film from the same point, all the machines will have run through the 800 feet by the end of the film.

There is no problem in getting separate pieces of equipment to run at the same speed. The problem lies in getting them to speed up and slow down in step. (Some of the methods used are detailed in the appendix under *Interlock*, the name given to this type of synchronisation).

The dubbing theatre will need three separate types of equipment which have to run in synchronism. They are a *projector*, a *magnetic film recorder*, and several *film reproducers*.

The projector is probably the piece of equipment most likely to give trouble. Since the picture film moves intermittently (and not at constant speed as in sound equipment), there is greater chance of it breaking. In order to correct mistakes in dubbing easily a system called *rock and roll* has been introduced. For this system, which will be explained in detail later, the equipment has to be able to run in reverse in synchronism. When this is happening the chances of

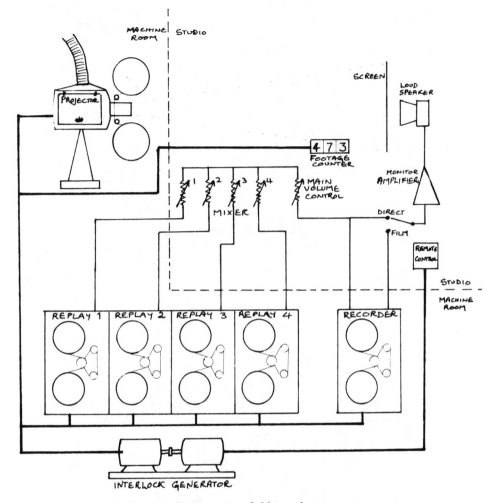

Schematic diagram of a dubbing theatre.

problems in the projector increase. The projector must therefore be of sophisticated design. On the whole this means that an engineer has modified a standard projector in such a way that it will take up film in reverse (not all projectors do this although most 16mm projectors do), and also run film in reverse through the gate (which entails reducing the pressure of the gate in order to reduce the friction on the film). It is also necessary to devise a system which blocks off the projector lamp while the film is stationary. Some dubbing theatres are able to show a dim picture when the film is stopped, a facility which is very useful. It is generally more difficult to get 16mm to run in reverse than 35mm, since 16mm is engaged on one side only thereby putting greater strain on the single perforation per picture. The *magnetic film recorder* in a dubbing theatre is very much the same as that in a transfer suite. It has to be able to

131

A bank of reproducers or 'dubbers' in a dubbing theatre. The upper ones are for 35mm and the lower for 16mm.

run in synchronism with the other equipment (in reverse too) and generally it is possible to playback from the record head (a facility called Selsync) as well as the replay head (this latter is a great help when using the rock and roll process).

The film reproducers, also called *dubbers,* are exactly the same as the recorder except they do not have record heads or amplifiers, or erase heads.

Both the film recorder and the reproducers will be able to run individually as well as in interlock, a switch selecting the function.

Coupled to the system which runs the projector, the film recorder and the reproducers in synchronism is a footage counter. This counts the length of film which has run through the equipment and must be able to work for both 16mm and 35mm film. It may also count time (24- and 25fps). It has of course to be able to work in reverse. The counter display is placed so that it is easily seen by the dubbing mixer, usually just below the screen, or at the top of the mixing desk.

There are two distinct electrical circuits in a dubbing theatre, one for synchronising the machinery, one for audio signals. The interlock circuit will usually be presented to the operator as a series of buttons: LOCK, FORWARD, STOP, REVERSE, RESET. There may be two sets, one on the mixing desk and one next to the piece of equipment most likely to give trouble, the projector. Because of this, in some theatres only the projectionist controls the motion of the film, the mixer communicating with him by a sort of engine room telegraph.

When a film is about to be dubbed, synchronising marks on the picture film and on the sound tracks are set in the projector gate and at the replay heads respectively. It is easier to do this when the machines are not in interlock because each machine can be 'inched' to get the synchronising marks in exactly the right place. When the dubbing process is started the interlock is engaged, which literally locks all the machines together. When the forward or reverse button is pressed, power is applied to the motors and they all run up to speed.

Other sources of sound signals may be provided in a dubbing theatre, such as turntables, tape recorders, cassette and cartridge recorders. These and the dubbers are all connected to a patch panel (just as in the transfer suite). The circuits for interlock and audio signals are kept separate in order to reduce to a minimum any chance of interference. Indeed it is usual to use metal box-section tubing, known as trunking, which provides extra shielding, to contain the wires. There is separate trunking for the interlock wires and audio signal cables.

The patch panel is normally situated next to the mixing desk where it is easily accessible to the dubbing mixer. The philosophy of the layout and operation of a patch panel depends on the design of the mixing desk. To define a mixing desk in its simplest terms—a device which enables the operator to combine many sources of audio signal in the volume proportions desired. But mixing desks have come to mean much more than that. They have become very complex devices which enable the operator to manipulate sound to a considerable degree. First of all the components of a mixing desk.

Volume controls. These are the basic, most essential part of a mixing desk.

LOCK	FORWARD	STOP	REVERSE	RESET		RECORD	CUT RECORD

LOCK: ENGAGES INTERLOCK BETWEEN PROJECTOR, RECORDER AND REPRODUCERS
RESET: BREAKS LOCK BUT ONLY WHEN ALL MACHINES ARE STOPPED

The controls you would expect to find on a dubbing desk.

They enable the operator to adjust the volume of the sounds which are being fed into the mixer. There are basically three different designs for volume controls (also called: potentiometers, pots, faders, gain controls). They are the *Slide fader,* the *Quadrant fader* and the *Rotary fader.* The rotary fader is out of the question for the film dubbing mixer since it is only possible to work one at a time with each hand. A fader that can be moved with one finger is much more useful, especially if the faders on the desk are close together since then it is possible to move more than one at a time with the fingers of one hand. It becomes possible to do, with one hand, what would take four hands with rotary faders. The quadrant and linear faders both fall into this category (see illustration).

Left: *Quadrant faders.* Right: *A pair of rotary faders.*

Three track headblock for 35mm film recorder. Left to right: erase, record and replay heads, each composed of three heads one above the other.

The simplest type of mixer consists of a series of faders, let us say ten, all coupled together so that they can combine ten separate sound signal sources into one output which can be fed into a recorder. This type of mixer would be known as a ten into one. There is often a need for more than one output from a mixing desk, for stereo and for three-track film recording. This latter is used when it is known that a foreign language version is to be made of a film sound track. The dialogue, music and effects are recorded on separate tracks on a roll of 35mm magnetic film. At a later stage, when the foreign dialogue has been recorded, the roll of film containing it is placed on a reproducer, and the three-track roll on another. The music and effects tracks only of the three-track roll are replayed with the new dialogue. Since they exist on the tracks in the correct volumes, there is very little mixing to do for the foreign version of the film. Each channel of the mixer therefore needs an output group selector enabling the dubbing mixer to route the audio signal from each source to whichever track he wishes. If the mixer had ten inputs and four output groups it would be known as a ten into four. There would be four extra volume controls known as group faders. This enables the dubbing mixer to fade out all the signals to each group separately. Connected to each output group is a meter, calibrated so that it reads the same as that on the film recorder.

This simple mixer is not enough for the dubbing of films. Frequently it is possible to adjust the tonal quality of the sound to match one section of a dialogue track with another, to produce effects like the sound of a telephone conversation or a transistor radio, and to remove unwanted noise. This requires the addition of a *filter*. The function of a filter is to vary the frequency response of a signal source. This should be done without otherwise affecting the signal—like adding noise or distortion. There are many different types and makes of filter. They all have similar features. Controls enable the dubbing mixer to adjust the strength of the bass, middle, and high frequencies relative to each other. For example it may be necessary to use an old gramophone record to give atmosphere to a film sound track. Without removing the hiss, the sound of the record would be awful. Since the crackle and scratch of an old record is mostly in the high frequency end of the spectrum, a filter is used which reduces the frequency response of the signal drastically in the high frequencies. Such a filter is also called a low pass Filter because it is removing all the high frequencies and passing all the low frequencies (called on a domestic amplifier, a treble control). Its opposite (the bass control) is a high pass filter. Traditionally these filters only cut the frequency response and do not boost the sensitivity in specified parts of the frequency range. Modern filters boost as well as cut.

The curves of a typical mixing desk filter are printed on the next pages. There are other types of filter worth mentioning. The *variable band stop filter* removes a very narrow band of the frequency spectrum, the frequency at which this takes place being adjustable. This filter is useful for removing tone and camera noise which may get on to the sound tracks from some source or other. For instance it is possible for the tachometer tone used to control the speed of the motor in a Nagra to get onto the recorded audio signal (if the Nagra is badly adjusted). This can be removed by a band stop filter which hardly affects the overall tonal quality of the audio signal. Skill is needed in the adjustment of the filter to the right frequency, a process that is helped if the dubbing mixer has some knowledge of the frequency of the sound he is listening to.

The *telephone filter* is a severe high and low pass filter which restricts the signal to a band from about 600Hz to 3KHz i.e. the bandwidth of a telephone. This can also be used to simulate a small portable transistor radio.

A *graphic equaliser* is a filter which is essentially a collection of amplifiers with limited frequency responses. If they are all set with their controls at the same setting then combined they have a flat frequency response. But the overall frequency response can be varied in a complex way which is sometimes useful for improving the quality of bad recordings. The name 'graphic equaliser' has been given to the device because of the similarity of its layout to a frequency response graph (see illustration on page 139).

TONE CONTROLS

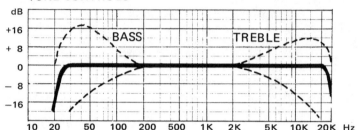

The dotted lines show how the frequency response is varied by the "bass" and "treble" controls

High Pass & Low Pass Filters

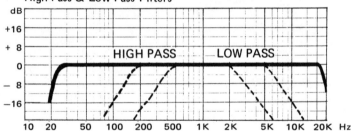

The dotted lines show the effect of high and low pass filters on a flat frequency response. The point at which the filter becomes effective can be selected.

Mid-Range Filter

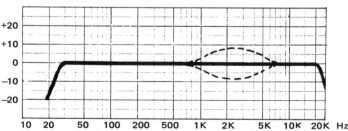

The dotted line shows the type of Boost and Cut which can be applied to a flat frequency response by a mid-range filter. The point of maximum effect can be selected. i.e. 1,2,5,8 KHz.

On the left a high, mid and low frequency filter, right, a telephone filter.

Taking the simple mixer a step further, it is necessary to find a way of incorporating the filters. Each channel is fitted with an insertion point. This is a break in the audio path of the channel which is taken to a pair of sockets in the patch panel. A switch normally connects the channel directly to its fader, but can be thrown to open the insertion point. The filters are also connected to the patch panel. If a filter is patched to the channel insertion point it will become effective when the switch is thrown. In other words the signal has to go through the filter in order to arrive at the channel fader. The gain of the filter is arranged so that it is unity and therefore does not affect the sensitivity of the channel.

Most modern mixers have separate filters built into every channel. Nevertheless each channel still has insertion points for the addition of the specialised filters like the telephone and band stop filters.

A small dubbing theatre capable of 35 and 16mm operation should be able to replay from at least four reproducers in each gauge. The reproducers may be dual-gauge, in which case there would be half the number. There would have to be two projectors, one 35mm and the other 16mm, which would be capable of running the picture and one sound track in synchronism (known as a double-headed projector). This would mean that facilities exist for playing back an extra track in each gauge. There would also be a 35mm and 16mm film recorder. If the studio has a need to record three tracks on 35mm film, there would have to be a separate three-track recorder. On its own the foregoing list of equipment makes up a versatile dubbing theatre. Additional equipment would include a tape recorder, (to provide replay facilities so that transfers can be made from tape to film, and film to tape), a turntable and cassette and cartridge machines (to provide additional playback of non-specific background sound effects).

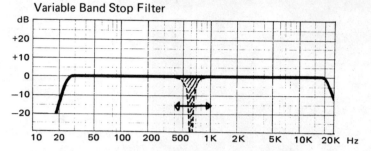

Variable Band Stop Filter

The shaded area indicates the band of frequencies removed.
The frequency at which the filter operates can be selected.

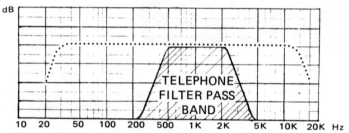

The shaded area indicates the band with the "Flat" Frequency
Spectrum which is passed by a telephone filter

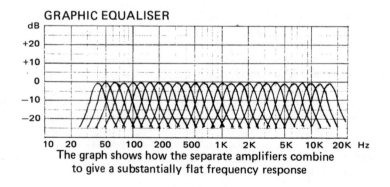

GRAPHIC EQUALISER

The graph shows how the separate amplifiers combine
to give a substantially flat frequency response

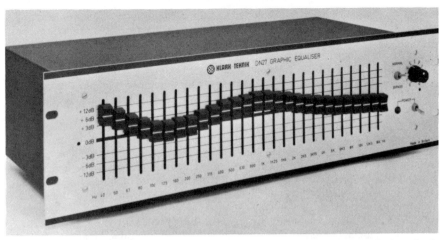

A Graphic Equaliser.   *Photo: Klark Teknik.*

The signal strength from all these different pieces of equipment will be roughly the same so that provided the recording is of reasonable quality the dubbing mixer will know the setting for his volume controls. If microphones need to be used, they will either be fed into microphone pre-amplifiers and from there to the patch panel or directly into the channel which will have to be switched to increase its sensitivity.

A switch enables the dubbing mixer to listen to the output of the desk or the output of the film recorder, known as a *direct/film* switch. In the process known as rock and roll, the connection between the film recorder and the film side of the direct/film switch is from the replay head when the recorder is in the record mode, and the record head, when the recorder is not in the record mode, a point which will become clearer shortly.

Dubbing started as a primitive system for adding sounds to tracks, sounds which had not been recorded on the floor. It developed quickly into a complicated process with sometimes as many as 40 tracks running at the same time. This was to a degree necessary because the recording was made photographically (optical sound). The photographic process is not reversible, nor are the results particularly good. The need for many different tracks arose because of the need to simplify the mixing, and because of the need to make a composite sound track without a further re-recording process. The mixing was simplified because there was one track devoted to each sound (dialogue for different actors, wind, water, motorcars etc) which could easily be located on the mixing desk, and further re-recording processes were avoided since the whole film could be mixed in one run. There would have to be at least three mixers, the chief mixer and two assistants, in order to handle the large amount of tracks, especially since they were handling the tracks with rotary volume controls.

To-day, with magnetic sound tracks there is greater flexibility. The magnetic recording process is reversible, and the track already recorded can be erased and recorded again. This means that if a mistake is made no stock is wasted. Therefore there is not so much need for long rehearsals. The process, now universal, known as Rock and Roll, enables the dubbing mixer to stop recording when he has made a mistake, reverse the picture, the tracks, and the master track in sync, to a point well before the mistake. When going forwards again the dubbing mixer compares the level of the signal at the desk with the signal coming from the replay of the recorded master track, by using the direct/film switch, and when he is satisfied that there is no difference between the two he starts recording again. The comparison involves listening carefully for the difference between the two different sounds. Since in dubbing there may be many different sounds running, there may not be much difference in the overall level but only a difference in one part of the whole sound. Sorting out which is which requires special listening skill which is aided by remembering which volume controls were moved or moving when the mistake was made.

It is necessary to listen to the replay from the record head during the rock and roll process so that the sound heard synchronises with that of the direct signal from the separate sound tracks.

The film recorder has to be arranged so that it will start recording without introducing a click to the recording. This is fairly simply done by ensuring that the bias does not come on instantaneously but rises gradually for about 200 milliseconds before reaching its full value. The fact that a short section of the track (the distance between the erase head and the record head) contains two signals, the original recording and the new recording, does not seem to matter. The question of whether or not there is a click at the point of re-starting the recording can be monitored by someone who is listening to the signal from the replay head of 'the recorder all the time. He is generally known as the sound camera operator, a hangover from the days when there was an optical sound camera. Some equipment is so good that there will never be a click when going into record, and the only thing that needs to be ascertained is whether or not there is a jump in level between the old and the new recordings. This can be done by the dubbing mixer if he is monitoring off the replay head. This practice is not favoured by many dubbing mixers since the sound will be out of sync with the picture. On the other hand there are a few dubbing theatres which purposefully thread the picture out of sync with the tracks. In this way it is possible for the dubbing mixer to listen to the replay head of the recorder all the time and still have the picture and the sound in sync. It is a bit of a problem, however, if he has to use the picture as a cue for any part of the mixing.

There is no need to run as many tracks now that magnetic sound is being used. The better quality of magnetic sound, especially the better signal-to-noise ratio, makes it possible to make, what are called pre-mixes. In this way the dialogue can be mixed down from the dialogue tracks. The single dialogue mix can then be run with the music and effects tracks and they can be mixed in. The advantage of this is that the dubbing mixer can concentrate on getting the dialogue tracks to flow from cut to cut, and get the perspective of the sound from the actors correct, without having to worry about all the other sounds. It is important that he gets the perspective right since once the decision has been made it is not possible to return to the separate dialogue tracks without a lot of trouble, although it is of course possible to make minor alterations during the final dub.

As mentioned earlier, it is possible to record more than one track on 35mm film. For monophonic sound there is little need for more than three tracks. If the tracks of the film have been laid so that they are well separated into dialogue, effects and music tracks, then these sounds can be recorded as separate tracks on the final dub. They will be recorded in their correct respective levels, so that when they are replayed on a recorder with three parallel replay heads, and mixed equally, the sound from the loudspeakers will be the same as the mix. There is usually a transfer process down to one track for double-headed preview and transfer to optical sound for subsequent printing. The advantage of using three-track is that what is called a music and effects track is automatically made. The M & E is recorded with the correct volume and perspective and with another track, containing a different language version of the dialogue, can be used for rapidly mixing a foreign version of the film. M & E tracks are also made without the use of a three-track recorder. Generally dubbing mixers like to mix them after mixing the whole film so that they can achieve roughly the correct proportion of effects-to-effects, and effects-to-music, from the previous experience of mixing the tracks with the dialogue.

Magnetic film reproducers are designed so that they can accomodate either a loop former or box. This device enables film to be run in the form of an endless band. A sound effect like traffic, atmosphere, etc. can be run as a continuous effect. This means the economy of not needing to lay the effect into the tracks thus saving the tracks for spot effects. The other economy is that a long length of the effect does not need to be transferred if it predominates in a reel of film. The disadvantage of loops is felt when an effect like a ticking

35mm loop box for running endless lengths of film. In 35mm these can run for long periods without attention, but with 16mm there can be difficulties due to the smaller dimensions of the film.

clock is used. Generally loops run best if they run forwards only. Therefore they are switched on and driven continuously during a dub—they do not rock and roll with the tracks. If it is necessary to roll back to correct a mistake there is every chance that when the dubbing mixer starts to record again, that the clock will be in the wrong place relative to the clock on the previous recording and that the effect will suffer from the "tic, toc, tic, toc, toc, tic, toc etc." effect previously encountered in editing. The same effect can be equally found with traffic, wind, sea, and is only overcome by skillful juggling on the part of the dubbing mixer.

Loop formers are limited in their capacity but are very suitable for 16mm. The loop box is ideal for 35mm and can take up to 200 feet with no difficulty. When a 16mm film is being dubbed, the loops needed can be run on spare 35mm reproducers. Some dubbing theatres transfer loops to half-hour cassettes, and run these instead, thus freeing all the film reproducers for tracks which have to run in sync with the picture.

Post-Synchronisation and Commercials

Loops are used for post-synchronisation and for the dubbing of short films like commercials. The reason is that in these processes there is a need for the rapid repeat of the film in order to get many chances of working on the film without the need for rewinding or rolling back. For commercials a metallic tab is added to the film (usually the picture). As this tab passes a particular part of the projector it resets the footage counter to its start footage thus giving the mixer footages every time round. It is important in all loop work that the loops be all the same length (exactly the same length) and that in 35mm the picture be spliced together so that it is always in rack.

Automatic footage counter zeroing: when the tab on the film reaches the roller on the left of the photograph it will complete a circuit which returns the footage counter to zero.

Post-Synchronisation

When shooting in noisy locations it may only be possible to record what is called a guide track. This is a rough recording which will be used later as a guide for editing, and for actors who will post-synchronise the lines in the studio, by speaking in time to their lip movements on the screen. In order to get rapid familiarity with the lines, the actor must have as many opportunities as possible to see the picture and hear the guide track. Hence the easiest way to approach the problem is to use loops of the picture and the guide track (exactly the same length) and allow him to practice on these. When the actor is happy that he can do the lines for the shot he says so to the dubbing mixer and they record on a new loop, known as a virgin loop, which is on the sound camera (magnetic film recorder) and which is exactly the same length as the other loops. (The guide track will have been fed to the actor on headphones so that the mixer can get the correct balance on the mike during the rehearsals, and will probably be switched off during the recording so that the actor can concentrate, and to minimise the chance that the mike might pick up sound from the headphones.) When the actor has managed a take which the mixer and the producer are happy with, the recorder is switched to replay and the loudspeaker in the studio switched on, so that all can hear what the performance was like. Again the film recorder must be able to replay from the record head so that the sound will be synchronised with the picture. Experienced actors are surprisingly quick at giving a good performance, but if the take was unsatisfactory it is a simple matter to start recording again and erasing the previous take. If the take was good but it is thought that a better take could be obtained, another loop could be used. On the other hand, if the film recorder has three-track heads in it, then the dubbing mixer can switch to the second and then the third track. A later transfer will produce versions of the takes on track one which is compatible with the editing equipment.

There are systems which do away with loops. The basis for the system is that if the film can be rolled back at higher speed and cycled accurately over the same loop of film time and again, then the time lost during reversing more than makes up for the time taken to break the film down into loops. It also saves on re-assembling the film afterwards. The equipment is however very expensive, and there are not that many dubbing theatres fitted in this way.

By post-synchronisation it is possible to recreate a complete sound track for a film. The system is not perfect since the sounds frequently sound phoney. A large dead studio is ideal for the job since it is possible to get the mike at a distance from the actor which approximates the distance used in actuality. A small studio, or speech booth, will impart a presence to the sound which is unreal. Exteriors are extremely difficult because of the unique properties of sound recorded outside. In the studio it is useful to have portable screens which are constructed with a hard surface on one side and a sound absorbent surface on the other. These can be used to change the acoustics around the mike at short notice. The dubbing mixer determines by looking at the picture, what the sound should be like, how far away it should sound, and how it would change during the shot. Someone in the shot approaching the camera would naturally get louder. To achieve this effect, the actor moves closer to the mike during the take, or in some cases the mixer adjusts the volume. It depends on what sounds best—I cannot emphasise that point enough. The studio will also be fitted with all sorts of floor surface. These are usually underneath strips of carpet which are moveable. Concrete slabs, parquet, hollow boards, gravel and sand are typical. If they are not part of the floor then a box which can be moved around the studio will be available. (For such things as walking down stairs, the foot movement which produces the best noise is a toe-heel action). For walking through long grass or on dry leaves, a bundle of old quarter-inch tape makes an excellent substitute. How accurate the footsteps need to be depends on what else there is on the tracks. Frequently the dialogue covers any mistakes. Movements like the little noises that clothing makes are an important part of post-synchronisation. These are made by rubbing one's hands over one's clothes. Woollen garments seem to be best for this since they make little noise unintentionally but a good noise when rubbed intentionally.

If at the dubbing stage of a film it is discovered that there is a sound missing which would add much to the action, it is convenient for a member of the crew to be able to record the sound quickly. This is usually a movement sound, possibly missed because of a mute take. Rock and roll is quick enough for this type of thing provided that the temporary actor is quick on the mark. This applies too to the dubbing mixer. In this case though the mixer has the advantage of knowing the other sounds, and can therefore assess the importance of the sound and its need for synchronisation and authenticity.

It will be seen that post-synchronisation is a complicated process relying greatly on the skills of both the technician and the artist. Modern equipment

Panels removed from the floor of a dubbing theatre reveal different surfaces for recording footsteps.

has made the technical side easier and has thus made it possible for the mixer to concentrate more on the sound obtained. No matter how easy post-synchronisation may be, there is a strong case (both aesthetic and economical) for getting the right sound at the time of shooting. This may be aggravated by such problems, on location, as waiting for the sun to come out. The sound recordist should therefore make every possible provision to cover, by making wild recordings of dialogue and all the sound effects which may be needed for a shot.

Echo

There are three ways to add echo to recordings artificially.

(1) A sound-proof room is prepared with extremely reflective walls plastered and painted with glossy paint. A loudspeaker is placed at one end and a microphone at the other. The reflective walls cause the sound waves to bounce around the room before losing their energy. Inevitably the microphone picks up the reflections one after the other. The result is echo.

(2) A spring is suspended horizontally in an insulated box. The signal to which echo has to be added is injected into one end of the spring by a transducer. The transmitted vibrations are picked up by another transducer at the other end of the spring. The signals fed in are not only delayed but are also reflected back and forth along the length of the spring adding to the echo effect.

TRANSDUCER
VIBRATES SPRING

TRANSDUCER SENSES
VIBRATION IN SPRING.

Spring echo: the spring, inside a box which is protected from external vibrations, is vibrated by a transducer at one end. The vibrations travel down the coils of the spring and are picked up at the other end by another transducer. The echo is compounded by the reflections of the vibrations within the spring.

Similar in operation but far superior and more expensive than the spring is the plate. An absolutely flat plate of steel, carefully suspended and damped is used, transducers feeding in and picking up the sound waves.

(3) A magnetic recorder can be used to create echo. The signal to which echo has to be added is fed to the recorder. The replay signal is mixed with the signal and the sound is therefore recorded again. Depending on the strength of the re-recorded replay signal, echoes of varying length can be made. If the replay signal is stronger than the original signal a feedback situation is reached in which the sound builds up to the point where a deliciously distorted effect is created. The speed at which the recorder is running and the physical separation between the record and replay heads affects the quality of the echo.

To make it possible to add echo to certain sounds only, the mixing desk has a separate mixer. Each channel has its own separate volume control called ECHO SEND which enables the dubbing mixer to send echo from a specific channel to the echo device. A further volume control called ECHO RETURN is used to mix the echo back into the desk. The echo is usually added to main signal and only very occasionally is it pure. Some mixing desks have a switch which enables the operator to select whether the echo send signal originates from before or after the main channel fader. If the echo is to fade in and out with the main sound the source of the echo signal must come from after the fader (post fader).

The dubbing process is complicated. The dubbing mixer, the person most involved in the process, has to be able to watch the picture, listen to the sound, watch the cue sheet and footage counter, work the various controls, as well as make decisions about how to get the best soundtrack for the film. He therefore has enough to do without having to worry about the equipment in the projection box. It is important that there is a team working in a dubbing theatre, and in a sense those who work the equipment are just as important as the dubbing

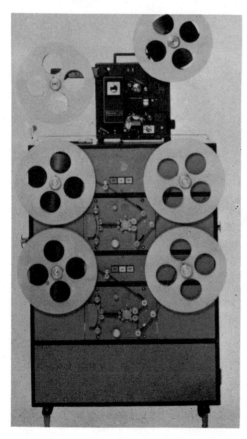

The PAG mini rack. There are two more magnetic film transports on the other side; all four are mechanically linked to the projector. The Mini Rack can provide four replay channels or three replay channels and one record channel for use in small TV or campus dubbing theatres.

Photo:
PAG Films
Ltd.

mixer. The way in which a film is prepared for dubbing is a vital part of the process and is described in the next chapter.

Since I wrote the above chapter I have had the dubious privilege of sitting in the dubbing mixer's chair. It was a salutory experience in the field of observation, not only of one's own concentration and ability in this respect but also of other people's, the editors and directors who sit next to the dubbing mixer during the re-recording process. Different people have different ways of describing what they want, and it is sometimes surprising how inadequate film people can be in using the English language.

The dubbing mixer has to be a curious mixture of artist, technician, diplomat and master of tact. If occasionally they throw pencils around, swear, walk out and generally become irascible, then this is not surprising, in my opinion.

Chapter VIII

Preparing a Film for Dubbing

Excellent books are available on the subject of editing. I do not pretend to be able to cover the subject better than they do. On the other hand what will be covered in this chapter are the aspects of editing which affect the dubbing process.

The Tape Joiner

Unless the splices are good there will be audible drop out when they go through the heads in a film reproducer. The splices for sound film are made with sticky tape, as indeed are the splices for the picture film. Probably the most convenient joiner to use for this is the Italian C.I.R. joiner (see illustration). There must be very few people who have read the instructions for

A C.I.R. 16mm film joiner, which uses sticky tape to join film.

Left: *When cutting for diagonal joins it is important NOT to press the film down in the space next to the cutter as this will mean that the cut is not being made in exactly the right place.* Right: *Before cutting the sticky tape stretch it across the film, this ensures a clean edge to the film when joined.*

the operation of these splicers—I have hardly ever seen them being used correctly. There is no doubt that if they are used properly and kept clean that they will make excellent splices for a considerable time. Here are some points relative to the use of these joiners.

(1) Keep the area where joining takes place covered with sticky tape, replacing it about every 100 joins. The sticky tape keeps the pins of the perforating punch clean.

(2) Stretch the tape across the film before pressing it on to the film. The fact that the tape is tight makes it easier for the knives that trim the edge of the film to cut.

(3) After using the cutting knives which cut the film leave them down.

(4) Make an especial point of leaving the knife which makes the 90° cut down. There is a great temptation to press the film down near the cutting edge while slicing the film. When the 90° knife is up, and a diagonal cut is being made, the film can easily be pressed into the space left by the knife. This increases the distance between the register pegs and the angled knife, and a join which has a slight overlap is made, and this will not flow smoothly past the replay head in the reproducer.

The joiner should be kept clean in the following ways:

(1) Unscrew the knurled knob around which the lever pivots. Press down on the part which carries the punches and edge trimming knives, and in this way reduce the tension on the shaft so that it can be pulled out. At this point various parts of the splicer may fall out.

(2) Set the handle, its shaft and knurled knob, and the small plate which is rounded on one face to one side.

(3) Gently lift the carriage which has the punches and knives off the two posts which guide it.

149

(4) Using a match and some solvent like alchohol, clean away the accumulation of adhesive and tape. Sometimes it is necessary to get at the insides of the blades. They can be unscrewed and removed for cleaning. There is usually a red dot which indicates the way in which it should be replaced. To replace the blade section, remove the springs from the pillars and gently lower the carriages on to them, so that the perforating punches enter the holes in the splicing surface. The whole splicer can now be used for lining the blades up in the right place. *On no account remove the perforating pegs.*

(5) Re-assemble the joiner using the reverse procedure.

Splices must be made without an overlap and if possible without a space between the two pieces of film. As with tape, all sound film splices should be diagonal.

16 mm C.I.R. joiner in pieces.

Spacing

Sound tracks for film are not made entirely of magnetic film stock. Old photographic film stock is used to fill up the spaces between the sections of film stock. This is called spacing. Wherever possible the spacing should have the same *perforation pitch* (distance between the perforations) as the magnetic film stock. If it does not, there is a chance that there will be a short time after the change from spacing to magnetic film and vice versa when the speed of the film going past the heads in a film reproducer will be different. This causes wow which is especially audible on 16mm film. There are examples of this effect on television almost every day, the worst offenders being bells, clock and telephone.

The most important point about spacing is that the emulsion of the spacing should always be spliced into the sound track so that it does not come into contact with the replay heads in the reproducer. If it does, the emulsion will be rubbed off by the friction of the head and build up on the head causing a loss

150

of contact between the head and the emulsion of the magnetic film with consequent loss of quality. The emulsion can usually be seen since it has a matt finish in comparison to the base. If there is any doubt the film should be placed between the lips. The sticky side is the emulsion. *The emulsion of the spacing must not come into contact with the head in the reproducer.* I cannot stress this point enough. I have seen a dubbing session stopped completely by this mistake. Moreover since the splices on the sound track are diagonal, it is not just a simple matter of turning all the spacing over, because a frame is lost at each end of the spacing with consequent loss of synchronisation.

Track-Laying

Track laying and dubbing are inseparable. The quality of the final sound track depends to a large degree on the understanding that the editor has for dubbing. There are some conventions which must be observed.

At the dubbing theatre the film in the reproducers needs a certain amount of time to run up to speed. This is because of the time taken for the film to drive the flywheels in the reproducers up to speed. The recorder also needs time to get up to speed if recordings are to be made which do not have any wow and flutter. It is therefore necessary to provide the film and its associated sound tracks with a leader which is long enough to allow all to reach the correct speed before recording starts. Then there is the problem of ensuring that the footage counter reads the right footage while the film is being dubbed. Generally about 20 feet of 35mm, and 10 feet of 16mm, are needed in order to get the dubbing session started.

The Sync Mark

The picture roll and the sound track rolls have all of them to be started from the same place in order to maintain synchronism between them. The roll of raw stock on which the recording is being made has to be marked with a sync mark too, so that it can be replayed in synchronisation with the picture after the film has been dubbed. The picture sync mark is a cross, the points of which define the corners of the frame. This is important in 35mm film since there are four perforations per picture and therefore four different places at which the sprocket can engage the frame. If the correct ones are not chosen, the picture will appear on the screen out of rack. The sync mark for the sound consists of three parallel lines across the film, the outer two of which define the frame, and the middle one the point where the gap in the head should lie. To either side of the marks, and along the length of the film a line is drawn. The function of this line is to tell the operator loading the film into the projector and reproducers, that there is a sync mark, which he is looking for, in the vicinity.

The distance between the sync mark and the beginning of the film is important. There are many standards, the best of which is probably that set by the old Academy leader—15 feet for 35mm and 6 feet for 16mm. The start of the film is the point at which either the sound or the picture start—or the point at which both start.

Establishing these parameters is not difficult. The equipment used is a synchroniser, or better still, a picture synchroniser (Picsync). This device consists of a series of sprockets on the same shaft and equipped with guides and rollers which hold the film. The picture sprocket has a rotating prism inside it which projects the picture through a system of lenses and mirrors onto a small screen.

Picture Sync Mark

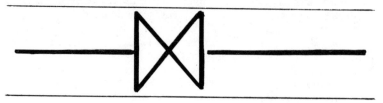

Cross defines corners of frame.

Sound Sync Mark

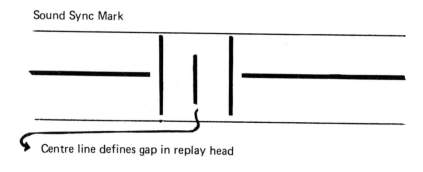

Centre line defines gap in replay head

Lines down the centre of the film warn the dubbing theater operators of the presence of a sync mark

The picture and the tracks can be driven through the synchroniser by hand or motor. The point about the apparatus is that since all the sprockets are on the same shaft, they must all turn at the same speed and the separate pieces of film must therefore be moving at the same speed and in synchronism. There is usually a footage counter to count the film as it is wound through, and the handle on the front of the device is calibrated in frames. The film is run from left to right.

The procedure for making the leaders for a film is as follows:

(1) Use Academy leaders wherever possible. If these are not available white spacing makes a good substitute.

(2) If Academy leaders are used there is no problem. Place them in the synchroniser, emulsion up, so that the sync mark lies on the sprocket on frame one. Set the synchroniser counter to zero and check whether the leader is truly 15 feet long. Sometimes there is more than one mark that looks like a sync mark. Work backwards from the sync mark and check that there is at least 5 feet of leader before the mark. This is important for loading the reproducers in the dubbing theatre. When white spacing is used the lengths will have to be

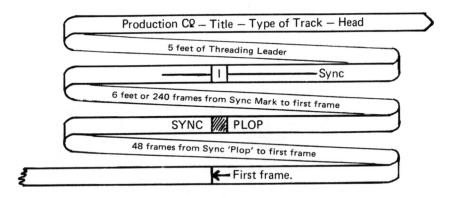

Dimensions of 16mm Dubbing Leader — Sync mark as for sound track

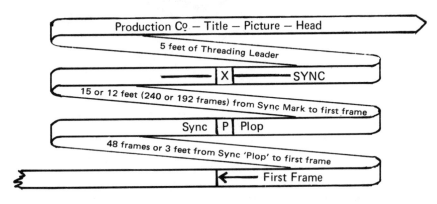

Dimensions of 35mm dubbing leader—Sync Mark as for picture
N. B. 12 feet from Sync mark to first frame coincides with
Picture start on Academy Leader

measured. Having placed the leaders in the synchroniser, set the counter to zero and wind through five feet. Find frame one on the sprocket and make a sync mark. Set the counter to zero and wind through 15 feet on 35mm and 6 feet on 16mm. Find frame one and mark the frameline between it and the preceding frame. This will be the point where the film starts.

(3) The leading end of the leader, called the *head,* must be marked with details of the film: the title, the reel number, the number of the track or the fact that it is the picture, and HEAD.

When the optical soundtrack is made of the mixed track there will be no indication of synchronisation. It is not possible to play the optical sound negative without the risk of scratching it, and if the sound track starts with a gentle fade in, it would be difficult anyway to find a synchronising point. At the laboratory where the film is being printed the technicians have never seen the film and are usually badly informed about it. It is therefore necessary to provide them with an indication of where to synchronise the optical sound negative to the picture. A

A pic-sync. This device allows the editor to run four sound tracks and one picture in synchronisation with each other. To the left of the screen are four volume controls so that the relative levels of the tracks can be adjusted. The sound quality is adequate for editing. This particular model is motorised.
Photo: Acmade.

single frame of tone (1 KHz) is spliced into the magnetic tracks, usually 48 frames before the start of the film; 3 feet in 35mm or 1 foot and 8 frames in 16mm. This is called the Sync Plop or Sync Pip and is used because it is immediately recognisable on an optical sound negative. It does not matter where it comes, provided that the laboratory doing the printing is informed of its whereabouts. TV producers tend to prefer to put it 4 or 5 feet before the start of the film (in 35mm) since this reduces the chance that it will be heard on the air.

(4) Find the frame where the sync plop is to go and splice it in, removing one frame from the leader (in order to retain the correct length).

Enlarged drawing of a sync plop. This is one frame of 1KHz tone in the leader of the film and it is used because it is so recognisable when the film has been transferred to optical.

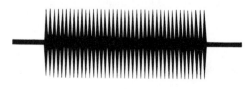

We will consider first of all the track laying for a simple film consisting of dialogue, perhaps in the form of commentary, and music. The picture has been edited and is therefore the right length. It has a title sequence and then the action starts. Over the title sequence there is music. The first note of the music is found and spliced onto the leader so that it starts at frame one, the picture and the music will therefore run through the synchroniser synchronised. The track which is to carry the commentary, has no sound on it yet and must therefore be filled out with spacing (with the emulsion away from the heads).

After the title sequence and the establishing shot the commentary starts. The first word of the commentary is found and joined onto the spacing. Now there are two tracks, music and dialogue and the picture running through the synchroniser. At the dubbing session the music will be faded down under the commentary. Now in all probability, the commentary will have been recorded wild (without the picture), and the spaces between the blocks of speech will not be right to maintain synchronism. There may also be out-takes which have to be removed. If this is the case it is probably better to drop the music for a while and concentrate only on the commentary. Let us say that the next block of commentary has to be placed later in the track. Spacing will have to be used to fill in the gap. Find the beginning of the next block of commentary without taking it out of the synchroniser, mark it and cut it. Make the cut on the left hand side of the synchroniser. This is because the right hand side is synchronised. Join on the spacing, emulsion away from the heads, and wind through to the place in the picture where the next block of commentary starts, and join it to the spacing.

In this way the commentary is synchronised to the picture. The two may well be run on a double-headed projector or motorised editing table to check the relationship between picture and sound. If it is found that a piece of commentary is late, it can be moved by removing some spacing from before it. However the spacing must be replaced after the section of commentary if the synchronisation of all the other commentary is not to be affected. *When altering the synchronisation of a section of sound always replace what has been removed.* In other words it is not the sound that is moved but the spacing. As usual the work is carried out on the left hand side of the synchroniser and the spacing is put back in to the tracks so that the emulsion is away from the heads.

The music may not be long enough to last the whole film. Alternatively, it may be desired to change the mood half way through. (Mercifully films are no longer made with music and commentary tracks only.) Obviously unless the music is continuous or an excellent cut can be made, there will have to be a cross fade between the two pieces of music. Another music track, consisting of spacing until the new music is to come in, has to be laid. At this point in a dubbing session, the dubbing mixer would fade out the first track while fading in the second. It is a good idea to lay far too much overlap so that (a) there is no chance of the first music cutting out during the fade out or the second music cutting in during the fade in, and (b) so that the dissolve between the two can be moved forward or backwards if it is felt that a better result can be obtained.

Let us say that a section of the film has an interview with a member of the public. The sound track for this should be laid on a separate dialogue track. This means that once he has set the filters and volume for both the commentary and the sync dialogue the dubbing mixer will not need to do any further

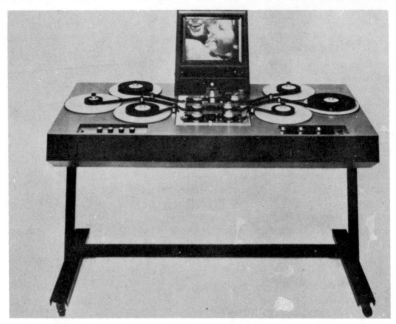

A six-plate Moviola editing table. Two sound tracks can be run in synchroni-sation with the picture.

adjustments. Every time there is a change the dialogue will go through the channel which is set up for it, as will the commentary.

At the end of the film the music will be increased in volume and come to an end when the end title fades out. To lay this section of sound track it is necessary to start at the end of the film and music and lay it into the tracks backwards.

So there it is, a simple (if rather awful) sound track consisting of two dialogue tracks and two music tracks. Simple though they may be, to the dubbing mixer, who has never seen the film before, the tracks might be very complicated. To provide him with information about the tracks a dubbing cue sheet is drawn up. This is a chart containing details of the tracks; the footages at which they fade in and out, the first and last lines of dialogue in each block of speech. (see illustration).

It will be seen that a decision has to be made about where to start the footage counter. It is convenient to think of the start of the film as being zero. This means that (assuming the dubbing theatre has a three digit footage counter) the footage counter will read 985 (35mm) or 994 (16mm) on the sync mark. When the film starts running the counter will reach 1000 for the start of the film, which, since there are only three digits, will show as 000. Some dubbing theatres are equipped with a button which will set the footage counter to these numbers automatically, so it can be seen how important it is to have the length of the leaders measured correctly; on the other hand some dubbing theatres find

156

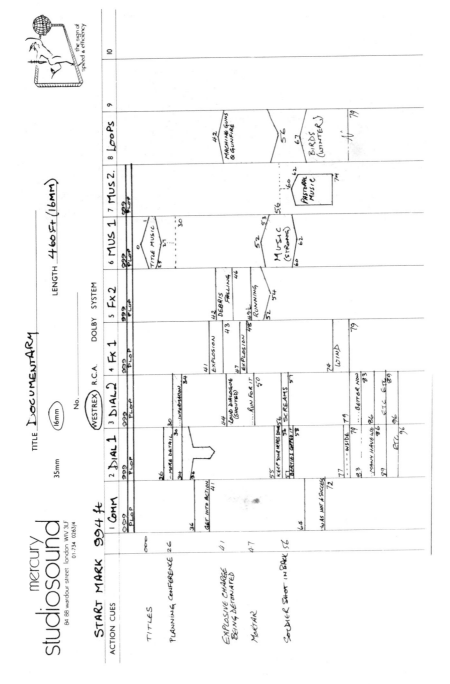

157

A dubbing theatre footage counter displaying 985, the start footage for 35mm dubbing.

it easier to start the counter at zero at the sync mark. The editor should find this out before going to the dubbing theatre. The one advantage of starting with the sync mark at zero is that there are no problems if the length of the leaders is collectively wrong, since both editor and dubbing theatre are definitely working to the same standard. The footages in a dubbing cue sheet should be to the nearest foot in 35mm and the nearest ½ foot in 16mm.

It is a well-established routine in making feature films to confine dialogue to dialogue tracks, music to music tracks and effects to FX tracks. This is less adhered to in documentary and TV film making which is largely 16mm and therefore governed by smaller dubbing theatres. In this case the music and FX tracks may be shared by different types of sounds. This makes it very important to write in each block on the dubbing cue sheet exactly what each sound is. Simple notes like traffic, flute music, barking, violin, will suffice.

When the dubbing mixer gets the dubbing cue sheet he will find out which reproducers have which tracks and will patch the appropriate machines into the channels so that the volume controls in the mixer are in the same order as the columns on the dubbing cue sheet. The convention is that dialogue tracks should be on the left followed by music and effects.

When a feature film has been edited, it can be viewed on a double-headed projector; however, since all the dialogue is on one track, it is not possible to overlap any of the lines, therefore the film is longer than it need be. Once the decision has been made to start laying tracks the final cutting can be achieved. The dialogue is kept as far as possible in the takes as they were shot. The assumption is made that the sound recordist has recorded the sound with the right perspective within each shot, and that when the editor has to cut from shot to shot, a certain amount of adjustment on the part of the dubbing mixer will have to be made. If the film was shot as a series of long master shots which just had to be joined together, then the tracks associated with those shots would be chequer-boarded; the odd ones on DIALOGUE 1 and the even on

DIALOGUE 2. The dubbing mixer would then be able to match the quality of the sound from one take to the next and provide a smooth flow of sound throughout the film (it has always interested me that we accept picture that is non-continuous; not so sound). Unfortunately the cutting of a film is hardly ever so simple. As a general rule, if a take has been split and action from two or three other shots introduced, it is better to put the sound from the extra shots on separate tracks, keeping the main shot's sound on one (so that the mixer can use a constant filter and level setting). Of course it is possible that the cut-ins are mute and the track continuous through them, in this case the track is not cut up. Once the dialogue tracks have been split up and the final cutting of the film decided they can be viewed and checked either individually with the picture in a double-headed projector, on a multi-headed editing bench, or indeed in a dubbing theatre.

It would really be better to call the dialogue tracks, sync tracks because they contain many synchronous sound FX such as footsteps, body movements and doors closing. Other FX may have to be added to these; for instance it is crazy to record dialogue with a clock ticking in the background since the level and quality of the clock will vary considerably from shot to shot, and the editor will be restricted because every cut he makes will be defined not only by the action and the dialogue but by his need to get the clock to go tic toc consistently, likewise dialogue in a bar must be recorded without music in the background.

The Sound FX Library

If the sound recordist has not recorded all the effects needed or if the character of the film has changed in editing so that the effects he recorded are wrong, the editor will have to turn to a sound effects library to get what is needed.

Sound effects libraries should be approached with trepidation. There is no substitute for the recordist getting the right sound while the film is being shot. A large sound effects library will contain thousands of FX. It is just a matter of thinking of how many different kinds of motor cars there are and how many different things motor cars can do, accelerate quickly, accelerate slowly, change up, change down, travel at 20, 30, 40, 50, 60 miles per hour, brake, skid, drive on tar, sand, gravel, hoot, idle, switch off, stall, cough, splutter and a host of other things. Doors too, motor car door, castle door, front door, swing door, sliding door; shut gently, slam, stick; yale lock, mortice lock, clunk click etc. The editor has to have a good idea of the sound needed because of the diversity and variety of sound FX available.

At the FX library there are usually facilities to transfer the selected effects to 16mm or 35mm. The individual FX are expensive but the transfer is usually included in the price.

Discs of sound effects are available, notably those from the BBC, which are copyright free. The user should check the label carefully in case copyright fees are due on the record. It is an infringement of law to copy any gramophone record and use it in a film unless there is a definite waiver on the label or permission has been obtained.

Track Laying (continued)

The next procedure is to make up a comprehensive sound effects track. What sound effects the editor chooses and how realistic he makes the sound effects track depends very much on the content and style of the film. For instance, if there is to be music laid over a section of the film there is hardly any point in making up a delicate sound effects track of quiet noises.

Any sound effects which are likely to recur frequently during a reel of film should be confined to one track. Instinctively the dubbing mixer will reach for that volume control when the track comes up. Effects should not be laid right next to each other. A rapid succession of sounds on one track is difficult to follow. The mixer may be making adjustments on other tracks at the same time. If the sounds are separated onto other tracks the mixer can preset the level for the sound while spacing is running through the reproducer and therefore be ready. There is therefore a definite rule about track laying—*never lay two different sounds next to each other.* In a complicated sequence where many short synchronised FX appear (spot FX) there may not be enough tracks to carry them. They can be laid on music or dialogue tracks if these are empty and the cue sheet clearly marked so that the dubbing mixer knows what is happening. Another rule—*when in doubt, lay another track* and—*never follow a fade out with a fade-in or cut-in, on the same track without leaving a five-second pause.*

Some sound effects, dialogue and music, cut in and out; this is alright if there is other information going onto the tracks, but if the tracks are very quiet then the cut-ins must have little background noise. Similarly if the background noise between blocks of dialogue varies, there will be a jump in quality at every cut. A good dubbing mixer will get over these jumps by dexterous use of the faders and filters, or by applying some similar background sound at the point of the cut. The editor can help by overlapping the tracks so that a quick cross-fade can be made. Of course, this can only work if there is empty track available. It may be possible to cover bad jumps in quality by the use of a sound effect like a car passing or a jet flying overhead.

It will be appreciated that there is little difficulty in running to 5 or 6 tracks for a documentary and many more for a feature film. The simple dubbing theatre described in the previous chapter could cope with a 6 track documentary quite easily by making a pre-mix of the dialogue tracks. These could be recorded on 35mm film since it is possible to run the 35mm recorder in sync (frame for frame) with the 16mm equipment. The only limitation may be the length of 35mm that it is possible to load on to the recorder (1000ft of 35mm = 400ft of 16mm in numbers of frames). Therefore the 35mm would carry the dialogue pre-mix and the four 16mm reproducers, would carry the music and effects tracks. Loops needed for continuous background FX could come off the 35mm reproducers as well as cassette machines.

Post Synchronisation

There may well be sequences or shots which for some reason or other may have to be post synchronised. These will be shots in which it was only possible to record a guide track in which the dialogue may be distant or smothered by inappropriate background noise. The actors are booked for the dubbing theatre, loops are prepared, and new lines are recorded in synchronism with the picture to replace those recorded in the guide track.

First of all it is necessary to decide how to break down the film into manageable sections for post synchronisation. These should not be too long. Wherever possible the sections should consist of complete sentences, and sentences, if they have to be broken up, should be broken at natural pauses.

160

Once the decisions have been made loops are made of the picture and the guide track. A leader is spliced into these loops. It has a sync mark and usually a countdown of 3, 2 and 1. On one of the numbers there will be a sync plop on the optical sound track. This sync plop is heard via the optical sound head in the projector and recorded in order to provide the editor with a sync point when he reassembles the film. At the end of the leader there is a wipe drawn on the film lasting about 1 second and which leaves the picture at the instant when the action starts. Wipes can be drawn on the action to indicate when a block of dialogue starts (the point where the dialogue starts arrives when the line leaves the side of the picture). A further loop, called a virgin loop, is made up from new magnetic film, and is used for recording the replacement dialogue. It goes without saying that all the loops must be exactly the same length. When more than one character speaks on a particular loop, two virgin loops are made up, one for each character.

At the dubbing theatre the loops are loaded into the projector, the recorder and a reproducer. When all is ready they are all run up to speed in interlock, the picture projected, and the guide track fed to the actor or actress either through a loudspeaker or through headphones. After two or three times through the actor will indicate to the mixer that he is ready to record (a professional actor can post synchronise dialogue extremely quickly). The speaker or phones are switched off, the recorder set into record, the plop recorded and a recording of the dialogue made. If the producer and the dubbing mixer are happy with the recording it can be replayed immediately for checking. If it can be re-recorded the next time around on a three-track 35mm recorder, it is possible to use the other tracks if there is uncertainty about whether or not to keep the take. If this facility is not available the 35mm film can be turned round and recorded down the other side.

Sound FX can also be recorded in this way, footsteps, body movements, horses hooves, glasses clinking etc; in fact there are people who make a living out of post-synchronising films.

Music for Film Sound Tracks

Music for films can be expensive. The reason for this is copyright. Music libraries are available, they have recordings of music of all moods (romantic, western, martial, chase, frontiers of space, electronic, pop, travelogue etc.) which can be used for a comparatively small fee depending on the projected distribution for the film. Selecting music from a mood music library can be frustrating, the titles of the numbers are very misleading, in fact it is sometimes the most inappropriate title which is best. It is a good idea to select the music during the editing process, so that if it seems desirable, the picture can be edited to the music.

On the other hand, the music can be written and recorded specially for the film. This has the advantage that the music can be written around the sounds which already exist on the track. The great Hollywood love theme with vibrant choirs of angels and serried ranks of strings is always reduced to a few quiet violins during dialogue scenes. It is almost impossible to fade down the full orchestra behind dialogue since it is too thick a sound (and sounds wrong when played softly). This sums up the advantages of specially recorded music over pre-recorded mood music.

The composer will probably be hired before the film is shot and will have

Neve dubbing desk at Pinewood studios.   *Photo: Rupert Neve Ltd.*

read the script. During editing he will see the film and start presenting ideas. How he writes the music will depend on the type of film and the budget allocated.

At the recording session the conductor, who is often the composer, will wear a headphone on which he can hear either the dialogue or a "click" track. He will be able to see the picture which will be marked up with wipes to indicate the points where music starts, changes mood or ends. The click track is a series of scratches on the optical sound track. They are spaced at regular intervals, a decision made by the editor and the composer, and give the conductor an idea of the tempo of the music.

Chapter IX

Optical Sound Transfer

Until the advent of optical sound recording, sound films were not really practical. Although the first patents for optical sound were taken out in about 1906 by Auguste Lauste, it was not until around 1930 that optical sound recording and subsequent reproduction in an auditorium became possible. Yet since then there have been few advances in the parameters for and the quality of optical sound; that is, until very recently, when the addition of the Dolby system has increased the signal to noise ratio and the frequency response.

In magnetic sound recording a signal is translated into magnetism and recorded on a medium that stores magnetism accurately. In optical sound recording the signal is made to modulate a beam of light, either changing its density or dimensions to produce an image of the sound which can be photographed on a moving photographic emulsion to produce a record of the sound recorded.

The huge advantage that optical sound has over the other medium that was tried for making sound films, the gramophone record, is that the sound record can easily be printed alongside the picture thus facilitating the repair of damaged prints, establishing a synchronism, and assuring that the correct sound and picture are exhibited at the same time.

There are two types of optical sound: variable density and variable area. Let us consider first the reproduction of optical sound. From the photograph it will be possible to see that a variable density sound track is one in which the changes in pressure in the atmosphere which constitute sound are represented by variations in density. These can be reproduced by shining a light through the moving track onto a photo-electric cell and thence as a signal to an amplifier. In order to increase the definition of the reproduction the slit must be as fine as possible consistent with passing enough light for the photo-electric cell. As with magnetic sound, the system does not make any sound unless the film is moving, providing a changing light intensity at the photo-electric cell.' The variable density system has a constant width and the amount of light that is passed is controlled by the density of the silver on the track. The system produces very good results but is very critical of conditions in the processing stage since the gradations of density between black and clear can vary according to the processing.[1] As a result variable density sound recording is no longer in extensive use.

In the reproduction of sound the variable area sound track has the same effect as the variable density sound track. Instead of varying the amount of light by varying the density of the sound-track area, the track consists of a narrow transparent area which is varied in width in accordance with the signal to be reproduced. Thus the track is high in density during quiet passages, and there is high contrast between the transparent and dense zones.

---

[1] Cf. "Photographic Theory for the Motion Picture Cameraman" by Russell Campbell, Chapter 3.

Sound tracks: top, Variable density, below, Variable area.

There are critical parameters in the reproduction of optical sound tracks (applicable to both variable area and density tracks) which require adjustment of film projectors. The adjustments can be made using test films, of which there are three different basic types:

(1) Buzz track. This is a test film which contains two tones recorded outside the area of the optical sound track. Each tone is of a different frequency, 300Hz nearest the picture and 1KHz nearest the edge in 35mm, 16mm being similar. The space between the two tones is opaque. Thus the position of the slit in the projector's sound head can be adjusted so that it scans the correct area of the film, i.e. not part of the picture or the perforations which would be heard as a noise.

(2) Azimuth Track. This is a high frequency recorded on the film to enable the azimuth and the focus of the slit of light which falls on the film to be adjusted. In both cases the adjustment is made by connecting a meter to the output of the projector. The azimuth and focus controls are adjusted separately to give the highest voltage at the output. When both adjustments have been made they should be done again, since the results obtained the first time around will be dependant on how much the equipment was out of adjustment. Some 16mm projectors have a focus control for the optical sound head which is easily accessible since in 16mm there is a dual standard for the position of the emulsion—either towards the lamp or away from it. Sometimes these controls are accurate enough to be marked with the two positions.

(3) Frequency response. A film recorded with a series of tones similar to a magnetic test track, containing frequencies from 40Hz to 10KHz (in 35mm) all recorded to the same amplitude. The two graphs show the frequency response of reproduction in 16 and 35mm projectors. This rather bad response is necessitated by the fact that the photographic emulsion has a grain structure which causes noise, as does dirt and scratches accumulated during use. (This can be rectified to a large degree by the addition of the Dolby Noise Reduction system, of which more later.)

Two types of instrument are used in the recording of optical sound tracks: The *mirror galvanometer* & the *light valve*. The galvo, as it is affectionately known by its supporters in the industry, is used by RCA in its sound cameras, and can only be used to make variable density sound tracks. It consists of a mirror supported by a tautly stretched metal band and balanced on an armature via a knife edge. The armature lies in a magnetic field created by permanent mag-

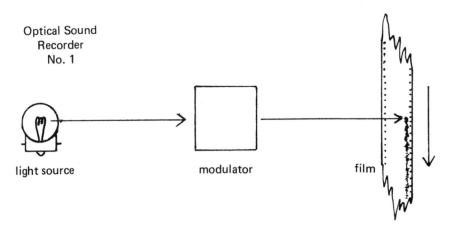

Optical Sound
Recorder
No. 1

light source   modulator   film

The essence of an Optical Sound camera. A beam of light is modulated so that it is analogous to the sound signal that has to be recorded, and then photographed on film that is moving at a constant speed.

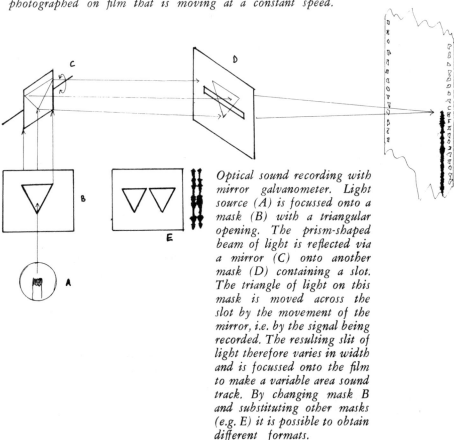

Optical sound recording with mirror galvanometer. Light source (A) is focussed onto a mask (B) with a triangular opening. The prism-shaped beam of light is reflected via a mirror (C) onto another mask (D) containing a slot. The triangle of light on this mask is moved across the slot by the movement of the mirror, i.e. by the signal being recorded. The resulting slit of light therefore varies in width and is focussed onto the film to make a variable area sound track. By changing mask B and substituting other masks (e.g. E) it is possible to obtain different formats.

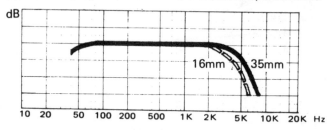

Approximate Response Curves for 16 & 35mm Optical Sound

dB

16mm   35mm

10 20   50 100 200 500   1K 2K   5K 10K 20K Hz

nets, and has two electromagnetic coils wound around it. Current passed through the electromagnetic coils causes the armature to move and thus tilts the mirror on the knife edge. A triangular beam of light is projected via the mirror and an optical system to a mask containing a slit, which in turn is focused onto the film. The image of the triangle is moved up and down relative to the slit which thus passes a band of light which varies in length according to the modulations applied to the coil in the galvo. It can be seen from the diagram that by changing the shape of the mask that creates the beam of light that is directed at the galvonometer it is possible to create different types of variable area optical sound tracks. Closer examination of the bilateral variable area sound track shows some of the problems associated with optical sound recording. The level to which the sound track is modulated is dependant on the physical limitations of the area available. If the modulations extend outside the zone which will be scanned by the slit of light in the projector the effect is one of clipping the peaks of the recording. This effect is not undesirable for very loud sounds such as gunshots where a certain amount of distortion adds to the effect. When the track is wide open it will be seen that there is a high likelihood that dirt and scratches which accumulate with the film's use will cause noise on the track. This is acceptable

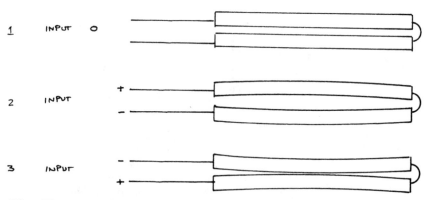

1   INPUT   o

2   INPUT   +   −

3   INPUT   −   +

The ribbons in a light valve are very small and delicate. They are mounted in a strong magnetic field. When no current is running through the circuit the ribbons are at rest (1). When a signal passes through the circuit the ribbons flex in the magnetic field, either moving closer together or further apart according to the direction of flow of the current (2 & 3). The varying gap between the ribbons is used to modulate the beam of light.

166

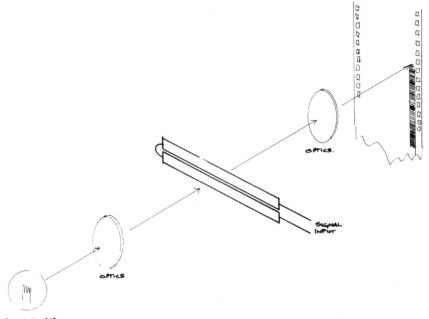

LIGHT SOURCE

The light valve used to produce a variable density sound track. This type of optical sound track is virtually never used.

The light valve used to produce a variable area sound track.

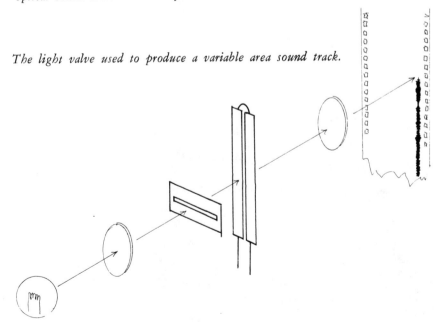

167

in passages where the recorded level is high and has a masking effect on the noise. But where the recorded sound is low in level it is necessary to close up the sound track as much as possible in order to reduce the clear area on the track. The current which performs this function, known as bias, is applied to the other coil, mentioned earlier.

The light valve, favoured by Westrex, consists, in its simplest form, of a wire under tension suspended in a magnetic field. Passing an electric current through the wire causes it to react to the magnetic field and thus to move. Two such wires parallel to each other can be caused to move towards and away from each other thus creating a gap of varying width through which light can be focused. This gap can be used to make both variable area and variable density sound tracks. The same problems of biassing and overmodulation apply.

Both types of optical sound camera have a system of optics which takes a

Westrex RA-13-10B optical sound camera. This equipment is well over twenty years old but still gives good service. 2000-ft magazines top and bottom contain the film, and the doors conceal the light valve and film transport illustrated on the opposite page.

The lamp on the left of the picture is focussed through the light valve, which is the square block in the centre. From there the modulated beam of light is focussed onto the film via a lens which is visible in the next photograph.

The film transport of a Westrex optical sound camera. The lens, which focusses the beam of light on to the film, can be seen on the left. The film that is being exposed is stabilised by the capstan next to the lens which is attached to a flywheel (not visible). The two sprockets on the right of the photograph drive the film.

small portion of the light from the transducer and passes it to a photo-electric cell, and from there via an amplifier to the sound camera operator. This enables him to compare the direct signal to that which is being sent to the film by the transducer (i.e. the galvo or the light valve). In a properly set up channel there should be hardly any difference between the direct and the PEC monitoring positions.

To prevent overmodulation there is usually a limiter in the chain. RCA favour compression as well as limiting.

Half the secret of recording good optical sound tracks lies in the regulation of the exposure, processing and printing of the film. Very fine grain blue-sensitive black and white emulsions are used, but in spite of this there is always some image spread caused by halation within the emulsion. Thus the ideal image as recorded by the transducer on the film does not truly exist on the negative, but is fringed as a result of the image spread. By carefully controlling the exposure and processing of the negative sound track it is possible to create a controlled amount of image spread which can be equalled· (but in the opposite direction) in the printing process thus to a large degree cancelling out the effect. The test to establish correct exposure versus processing and printing is known as a *Cross-mod Test*. This consists of recording two tones, 6KHz and 400Hz, mixed together.

Recording optical sound is a complicated process which requires skill and patience frequently laced with a bit of inspiration. As can be seen from the photograph of a sound camera there are many adjustments which have to be made; sometimes only slight, but enough to make the difference between a good and bad recording. Fortunately the process is excellently handled by experts who work in constant liaison with laboratories and obtain controlled and consistent results.

Chapter X

Recording

The sound recordist must know something of the processes which follow his work, i.e. editing and dubbing. They influence his work to a fair degree. That is why this chapter is at the end and not the beginning of the book.

Chapter 4 covers the handling of microphones; to summarise, the main aspect of microphone handling is the prevention of unwanted noises. To achieve this the microphone must be handled gently and isolated from vibrations (other than those caused by sound waves). Wind has to be kept away from the microphone diaphragm. Even when using a fish pole and studio microphone boom, care must be taken not to jolt or shake the microphone too much.

These precautions are necessary because it is bad to distract the audience from the content of the visible picture by unexplained sounds.

On the whole it is easier to get the microphone close to the source of the sound (without getting it into the picture) if it is on a boom of some kind or other. The boom swinger has to be able to judge how best to get the microphone close to the voice without getting it in the picture, reflected in any mirrors or picture frames which may be around, or its shadow in the picture. There is usually time to make this judgement while the shot is being set up, but frequently, especially with the modern tendency to use polystyrene sheets as reflectors, there is little space for the boom swinger to fit into. The fish pole is very convenient in these circumstances since it is small. It is a good idea for the boom swinger to stake his claim to the part of the studio where he wants to

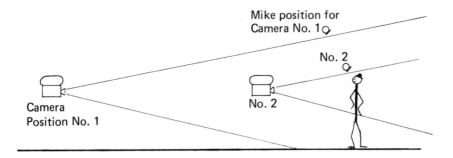

Microphone position is determined by camera framing. However, the distance of the camera from the subject in position 1 is massive compared to the distance of the microphone from the subject. When the camera is moved closer (position 2) the microphone is also moved in. The comparatively small movement of the microphone will have a large effect on perspective. Unfortunately for the sound recordist microphone position 1 would be useless in bad acoustics or where good quality sound is expected. In these cases a neck mike may have to be used.

stand before the lighting cameraman tries to fill it with reflectors or lights. As a general rule, the best place from which to put the microphone into a scene is on the opposite side of the camera to the key light (the main source of lighting for a scene). If the camera moves in closer to the character, the microphone can also be moved in usually by lowering. Likewise if the camera moves away, the microphone is raised to keep it out of the field of view. But the microphone cannot move away from the source of sound in the same way that the camera can. The subjective effect of distance increases far faster for a microphone than it does for a camera. The microphone cannot be attached to the camera in the hopes that since it is pointing in the right direction it will pick up the sound. The most important rule of sound recording is: *keep the microphone as close to the source of sound as possible* (within reason). When the subject moves and the camera remains static, the microphone also has to be moved. It should at all times be kept as close as possible and again raised and lowered in order to keep it out of the picture. The boom swinger, and good ones are rare, has to build up a special relationship of trust with the camera operator, so that both know that they know what they are doing and that the boom swinger is confident that the operator has this confidence and is letting him get the microphone as close as possible.

The boom swinger has to know the script well so that in scenes where there is movement, or scenes where there is dialogue between several actors, he knows when to move the mike. This is easy enough since there will be several rehearsals when his plan of action can be worked out, (a) as far as the sound is concerned and (b) as far as the camera operator is concerned.

The boom swinger has to think also about the clothes he wears. Since he is close to the mike he has to be silent, therefore noisy clothes like those made out of shiny leather or synthetic materials should not be worn. The boom swinger should wear soft-soled shoes. When working in a studio with a lot of lights, the boom swinger can get very hot, especially if he is perched high on a studio boom platform, and must take this into account.

He is responsible for the care of the microphones and the boom. From time to time a fish pole should be lubricated with furniture cream to make it easy to rack the telescopic sections in and out. The studio boom should also be lubricated but only with the recommended oils. Overnight and when not in use, the counterbalance weight should be removed and the tension taken off the strings which are used to manipulate the mike favouring and racking mechanisms.

Finally, the boom swinger must have excellent eyesight, for without binocular vision he is unable to judge distance, which is not conducive to good microphone placement.

The sound mixer (sound recordist) has the ultimate responsibility for the sound recorded for a film. He makes all the decisions relating to how the sound should be shot, and it is his knowledge of the editing and dubbing processes which will help him in this.

For instance, in a scene where two people are talking. This can be shot in several ways:

(1) The camera can be plonked down at right angles to the line between the actors and the scene shot with both actors the same distance from the camera.

(2) The camera can be placed first over one actor's shoulder and the whole

The author 'getting the mike as close as possible to the source of the sound.'
In a factory where there is a lot of noise it may be difficult to get the sounds
which seem to be characteristic of the machinery and many recordings should be
made in different places to try to capture the essence.

scene shot favouring the other. Then the situation reversed.

(3) The scene can be shot in big close up.

Indeed, in order to give the editor the material to build up a visually dramatic scene all three methods may be used.

It will be noticed that from (1) to (3) in the examples above the camera moves closer to the subjects. The microphone will be moved in closer too. But in methods (2) and (3) there is no need to record the dialogue of the actor whose back is to the camera. If the editor cross-cuts to favour the actor who is speaking then there will be clearly recorded sound available for the shot. If he uses one shot only and presents the other actor as a voice off, then that track is there too. But to shoot using this technique of favouring one actor only requires that the actors should not overlap their lines while shooting (the editor can do this later) and that the sound recordist should be listening all the time for such overlaps. In other words the recordist should know whether or not it is possible to separate the well-favoured recording from the bad (therefore the recordist should know something about editing sound).

If the previously mentioned two-shot situation is being recorded on location it is conceivable that some extraneous noise like a motor car or jet plane passing may ruin some of the lines of dialogue. The acting may have been perfect; the budget may not be able to run to another take; whatever the reason, if it is not possible to retake the shot, the dialogue must be recorded somehow. A good actor will be able to maintain the timing and nuances of dialogue from take to take. Therefore the shot is re-recorded "wild", without the camera running. With small adjustments the editor will be able to cut the lines into the tracks without losing synchronisation. In this way it is possible to avoid post-synchronisation.

Sound Perspective

There must be some kind of relationship between the distance a character seems to be from the camera and the sound that we hear. As said before if the microphone were attached to the camera and the camera moved away from the actor, the subjective sound change in distance would be far greater than that observed by the camera. It is for this reason that the microphone is kept as close as possible to the actor, and only moved vertically to get it out of the field of view of the camera. This small change in distance between the actor and the microphone is sufficient to give an effective change in perspective. Problems start to arise when one character is in the foreground and the other in the distance. If they are both in a room they would not necessarily be shooting at each other. The director may be using a very wide angle lens to accentuate a division between them. The sort of problems which arise in this situation are:

(1) How can the character in the distance be miked without getting the microphone into the picture?

(2) Should more than one microphone be used?

(3) If only one microphone is used can both the actors' lines be picked up either by favouring the microphone or by increasing and decreasing the volume control?

(4) If the volume control is increased will the mike pick up a lot of echo and extra background noise?

(5) If favouring the mike or adjusting the volume control will not work, where can an extra microphone be hidden to pick up the sound of the character who is in the background?

(6) Is it possible that since the character is so far in the background his lips won't really be seen and the lines can be recorded wild?

These are questions that the sound recordist has to ask himself, perhaps even try out during rehearsals, but which can only be answered by experience and trial and error. This is where the sound recordist's ear comes in to play. The more distant character should sound further away, which means that his voice should be softer and have slightly more echo (or ambience) than the closer character. Therefore if a second microphone is used it should not be as close to the distant character as the first is to the close character.

These problems are accentuated when working on location by such things as low ceilings and higher background noise than in a studio.

Matching the Sound from Shot to Shot

The sound recordist records a series of scenes which may be shot out of sequence. It is seldom that the scenes in a film are shot in script order. The editor will take these scenes and rearrange their order to make the final film. The recordist has to try to record the sound so that there is little or no difference in quality from shot to shot (with the result that the dubbing mixer will have less work to do to produce a smooth flow in the final sound track). The differences in quality can be summarised as follows:

(1) Level changes from shot to shot.

(2) Echo or acoustic changes from shot to shot.

(3) Level of background noise changes from shot to shot.

To a considerable degree the solution to these problems is in the hands of the boom swinger. If the microphone placing is on average a constant distance from the actors then the level will not change nor will the echo (unless the actors move into an environment with more echo, in which case the picture provides the reason for extra echo), and the background noise will remain roughly constant since the setting of the microphone volume control will remain untouched. It may be necessary to reduce the volume setting for loud patches of dialogue. On the whole, whispered dialogue takes place in close up, and it is therefore possible to move the mike close into the actors.

Recording on location always provides serious problems of background noise (especially traffic and aeroplanes); there is no simple answer to the problem (except to find a quiet location or shoot in a sound-proof studio). In some cases it is possible to stop the traffic for a time while the camera is running (but one can hardly stop aeroplanes). When it is not possible to stop the offending noise, the only solution is to try to get the mike as tight into the action as possible (hence neck mikes). A separate wild recording called an *atmosphere track* or *buzz track* should be made of the background noise, this can be used in the form of a loop by the dubbing mixer to cover up any gaps in, or differences between, the tracks. When recording an atmosphere track, the microphone setting and position should be the same as when the dialogue was being recorded. If the background noise is coming through the windows then its recorded quality will vary according to the direction in which the microphone is pointing, especially if a rifle microphone is being used. This is an additional cause of difference in quality between shots and can, to a degree, be solved by blocking off the windows (if they are not part of the scene).

Some locations are very sparsely furnished and produce too much echo on the recorded track, quilted *sound blankets* can be hung from the walls behind the camera to reduce the reflection of sound waves. Close microphone positioning again goes a long way to reducing the unwanted echo.

Other background noises like music and the ubiquitous clock must be stopped when recording dialogue so that the editor is only dependant on the dialogue for cutting and not on the clock or the music.

In the regulation of perspective certain sounds are a problem. Paper (for instance a letter) being unfolded always sounds louder on a recording than it does in real life. The cure is to have the writing on the paper done in indelible ink, and to keep the paper between damp newspaper until it is needed. The dampness takes the edge off the sound.

Noisy footsteps can be quietened by carpet if the feet are out of the shot, or by soft-heeled shoes. If neither cure is appropriate then self-adhesive felt of the type used for excluding draughts from windows can be stuck to the heels. This self-adhesive felt is also good for silencing noisy doors.

The above three sounds are examples of sounds which can be too loud in comparison to dialogue. If the door slam does not cover dialogue then it is possible for the recordist to dip the volume control momentarily instead. The essence is that he should be listening and recreating for the audience the subjective real sound.

Documentaries

Frequently a sound recordist is the only person working on sound on a documentary. This means that he has to look after every aspect of the job: recording, boom-swinging, keeping the sound reports. If these tasks are to be done properly and a good sound track produced, then the sound recordist has to be well organised. Let us consider the equipment that he may have around his neck.

A tape recorder weighing anything up to 20 pounds (approx 9Kg).

A microphone and its cable (and possibly a power supply).

A pilot tone cable to the camera (or crystal oscillator).

Report sheets and pen.

The weight of the tape recorder increases as time goes by.

The first thing that a sound recordist has to get to know is how to carry the equipment without tiring, what to do with the pilot tone cable, the microphone, and the report sheets while he is changing a roll of tape, and how to coil and look after the pilot tone and microphone cables between shots with only one hand, the other being used to carry the microphone. There are simple things which one can learn. For instance it is an idea to learn how to coil a microphone cable properly. Practice makes perfect and the process becomes easy so that in fact although one needs two hands it becomes automatic to tuck the microphone under an arm while coiling the cable. To avoid the need for too much attention to the microphone cable use a cable which is not too long. If it is too long then coil it up and attach it to the tape recorder with string or 'Velchro' which is glued back to back. Do not use camera tape as the adhesive comes off onto the cable making it sticky and liable to pick up dirt in an objectionable way. Report sheets can be kept in the lid of the recorder providing they are not too big. Some people write the details of the recordings on the lid of the tape box which they keep in the lid of the recorder. I like to have a terry clip attached to the case to keep my pen handy, and sometimes tuck the report sheet under the clip. To avoid getting a tired and sore shoulder from the recorder rest it on

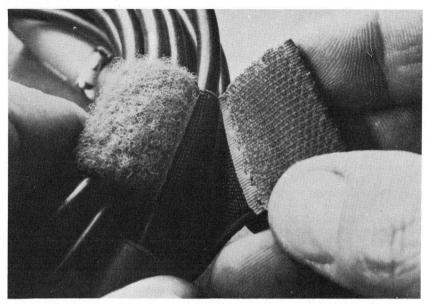

The author's method for tying microphone cables uses garter elastic and velchro, thus avoiding camera tape, which would leave a sticky deposit.

walls, motor car fenders, or anything as much as possible. Change the position of the strap across the shoulder, sometimes wearing it close to the neck and sometimes as far away as possible.

Wearing headphones all day can be tiring. I recommend leaving them off as much as possible except when recording. It is possible to lose one's perspective after a long time within the confines of the 'cans', besides which one should be listening to the real sound and comparing it with the recorded sound and in this way obtaining the best sound by adjusting microphone placement. On the other hand in a loud environment wear the phones as much as possible in order to protect the ears.

Know the tape recorder that you are working with. Be able to work it in the dark.

Finally, a good sound recordist is not one who tries to get a good or the best recording. The job, in my opinion requires that the recordist knows about the whole process of film making, knows how the director is thinking, knows the script, and above all makes a contribution to the style and content of the film through his or her own enterprise.

Chapter XI

Latest Developments

The Dolby System

Music studios have used the Dolby System for many years now for reducing the amount of hiss inherent in the recording medium, magnetic tape. They have found that the noise from the tape has become more and more of a problem since the advent of multi-track recording. The Dolby System divides the frequency spectrum into four bands and applies compression to each individual band during the recording process. When the tape is replayed the signal has to be decoded by a similar process, i.e. it is divided into the same frequency bands and then expanded. In this way the noise inherent in the tape is reduced in level during the quiet passages in the sound by some 10dB. Distortion and drop out are also reduced.

The Dolby System is not extensively used in film making. This is due to the quality of magnetic sound tracks being so superior to that of optical sound tracks. However, the Dolby laboratories have come out with a Dolby processor for optical sound tracks which has improved the reproduced quality of optical sound tracks considerably. More than that they have pointed out that part of the problem of reproduction in the cinema is the acoustics of the auditoria. Consequently, when installing a Dolby System into a cinema the acoustics are tested and a filter system installed in the amplifier chain which compensates the sound for the frequency response of the auditorium.

Some dubbing theatres have started to use Dolby for the dubbing process. The fact that not everybody uses Dolby is a problem, and unless it is known that the dubbing theatre which is to do the dub has Dolby it is not possible to transfer rushes using the system. A Dolbied track can be played on a double-headed projector without decoding, but sounds a bit strange. There are no problems in the editing process.

Problems do arise however when some of the tracks are Dolbied and others not and when they are joined into the same sound roll. When there is a mixture of Dolbied and un-Dolbied material never have them on the same sound roll for dubbing.

Stereo Dolby Optical

Because the Dolby process has improved the quality of the optical sound track so much (by increasing the signal-to-noise ratio and the frequency response considerably) it has become possible to squeeze into the sound track area of both 35mm and 16mm film two variable area tracks. The projectors have to be modified to read the tracks separately. The system is elegant in that the tracks recorded in this way can be replayed on a mono projector because the sound head will scan both tracks at the same time.

Stereo film dubbing is the province of the larger feature film dubbing theatres. The voices are recorded in mono in the normal way and then panned' across the picture during the dubb. The same applies to sync sound effects, but general atmospheres and music are recorded in stereo.

Digital Sound Recording

The problem with sound recording as we know it is that every time we make a copy of a sound track there is a deterioration in quality. This is because we are trying to make recordings which are magnetic analogues of the sound waves. In digital sound recording the sound wave is sampled, analysed, and converted into a series of numbers. It all sounds easy until one studies the number of numbers one has to record. Let us say that the highest frequency that you want to record is 15KHz. For this type of recording it is necessary to sample the sound signal at twice the rate per second as the highest frequency to be recorded, so that to get a reasonably Hi-Fi recording the signal has to be sampled 30,000 times per second.

For each sample there is a number which is a measure of the intensity of the sound wave at that particular instant in time. In computer terminology this number is called a word, and for the range of intensities it is necessary to record in order to get a reasonable sound and in order to encompass a reasonable dynamic range it is necessary to use a 13 bit word or a range of intensities of 4096 (2^{12}). Now the problem of recording binary encoded digital sound tracks should be evident: 30,000 x 13 bits per second = 390,000 bits/sec. This is the same as saying 390KHz. There are compensations in that it is not necessary to have bias because as long as there is something resembling a bit of information it can be replayed and decoded accurately. Binary encoded sound recordings have been made but the equipment is still very bulky. Binary encoded signals are regularly used in broadcasting for the transmission of sound over long distances without loss of quality.

Appendix One
The Nagra III Tape Recorder

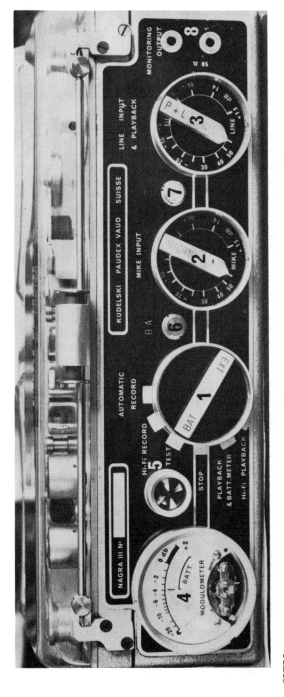

KEY:
1. Main Function Switch
2. Microphone volume control
3. Line volume control
4. Meter
5. Pilot tone input indicator
6. Tape/Direct monitoring button
7. Reference tone button
8. Headphone output
9. Microphone input
10. Deck Function Control
11. Tape feed tension roller
12. Tape take-up tension roller
13. Pinch wheel assembly
14. Erase head
15. Record head
16. Pilot tone head
17. Replay head
18. Capstan
19. Accelerator button
20. Flutter filter and 60Hz strobe
21. Flutter filter and 50Hz strobe
22. Feed spool spindle
23. Take-up spool spindle
24. Loudspeaker
25. Tape guides
26. Line input
27. Accessory socket
28. Line output
29. Pilot tone input
30. Speed selector switch

Description

The diagram shows the main controls of the Nagra III tape recorder. These are grouped on two surfaces of the machine, the deck and the front panel. Most of the time one uses the controls on the front panel. The *main function switch* (No 1 in the diagram) is used in conjunction with the *deck function control* (see No 10 in the diagram) to get the recorder to perform all its functions. We will therefore consider the function of each of these controls together and relate their functions to the other controls.

The Main Function Switch

This switch controls most of the electrical circuits in the recorder. It is a switch and has no mechanical connection to the deck. It has six positions, but can be turned through 180° to select whether the recorder is running on its own batteries or on an external power source. This is indicated on the switch by the letters BAT and EXT.

When the switch is horizontal the tape recorder is off. When not in use the tape recorder should be left in the EXT off position so that there is no chance of running down the batteries if the switch is accidentally moved.

Clockwise movement of the switch selects the test and record modes while anti-clockwise movement of the switch selects playback. When selecting a playback mode care must be taken not to move the switch beyond the two positions available, since, supposing one is using battery power, the third anti-clockwise position of the switch represents automatic record in the external power part of the switch. This switches the recorder into the record mode, and starts the erase circuits *even if there is no external power unit plugged in* since there is still sufficient power in the circuit. People who use the Nagra III for transfer sometimes fit a block into the switch so that it can only be turned to three positions, STOP, PLAYBACK, and HI-FI PLAYBACK.

We will return to this switch shortly.

The Deck Function Control

The deck function control is mechanically connected to the pinch wheel assembly (13) and in its most clockwise position engages the pinch wheel with the capstan (18). In its most anti-clockwise position it disengages the pinch wheel and connects the motor internally to the feed spool spindle to provide rapid rewinding of the tape. In the clockwise position the flutter filters (20 and 21) are pulled towards erase head (14) thus engaging the tape with this head and aiding in wrapping the tape around the record (15), pilot tone (16), and replay (17) heads. In the anti-clockwise position of the deck function control, the pinch wheel and flutter filters are pulled away from the capstan and erase head and thus the tape is no longer pressed against the heads which means that wear is avoided during fast rewind. It also means that when the tape is loaded into the recorder there is a straight path from the feed tension roller (11) and the take-up tension roller (12) making the recorder very easy to load.

The deck function control should always be left in the position where the two dots coincide when the recorder is not being used.

The Main Function Switch: Test

In this position the amplifiers of the recorder are switched on but the motor is not and thus a recording is not being made. The microphone input (9) is made live so that if the microphone volume control (2) is turned up it is possible to hear the sound being picked up by the microphone on headphones plugged into the headphone output (8), and it is possible to see on the meter (4), the strength of the signal that would be fed to the tape in the event of the recorder being switched to record. The line input (26) is made live and its sensitivity can be adjusted by the line volume control (3). Signals from the line source are also fed to the headphone socket and the meter. There is also a line input built into the accessory socket (27) into which can be plugged a mixer (designated BM, and, when fitted with microphone input transformers BMT) or a microphone pre-amplifier (designated BS) both of which take their power from the Nagra via the accessory socket. The line volume control acts as a master volume control for the mixer and if it is set on zero will give the inputs on the mixer the same sensitivity as the microphone input on the recorder.

If pilot tone is being fed into the pilot tone input (29) the pilot tone indicator (5) shows up as a cross.

Hi-Fi Record

When the main function switch is moved to HI-FI RECORD the motor of the recorder is switched on, the bias oscillator feeds erase current to the erase head and bias to the record head, and the headphone output is disconnected from the input of the recorder to the replay circuit, making is possible to hear the sound after it has been recorded. The BA button (6) enables a comparison to be made between the direct and the replay signals. The reference tone button (7) is made effective since it takes the tachometric tone from the motor, and which is therefore only present when the motor is running. By pressing this button it is possible to record tone on the tape, the level of which is adjusted by the line volume control. An indicated level of zero on the modulometer is equal to 320nWb/M or +8dBm. The frequency of the tone is approximately 4KHz at 15ips, 2KHz at 7.5ips and 1KHz at 3.75ips.

Automatic Record

This position on the main function switch in the Nagra III is to be avoided. The control of the volume setting for the microphone input is taken over by a compressor limiter of dubious design, producing unacceptable results. All other functions are normal.

Playback and Batt. Meter

In this position of the main function switch the recorder can be made to playback sound through its own internal loudspeaker (24). The volume of the sound from the speaker is controlled by the line volume control (3). *Warning:* on earlier models of the Nagra III be careful not to turn this control above '0' on its scale in PLAYBACK AND BATTERY METER since this can damage the loudspeaker amplifier. The strength of the signal appearing at the line output (28) is affected by the line and playback volume control (3) but the headphone output is not (8). This continues to produce the same level signal as it did when the recording was made. The quality of the signal available at the line

183

output (28) is not absolutely good and therefore it is not recommended that transfers from the Nagra III to other recorders be made with the main function switch in this position. With the deck function control (10) in the rewind (fully anti-clockwise) position power is transferred to the feed spindle (22) and the tape can be rewound.

The meter (4) reads the strength of the batteries or the strength of the supply in EXT. The needle must fall within the scale marked BATT. Although it is only possible to check the strength of the batteries in this position of the main function switch there is another warning. When the batteries no longer gave sufficient power to drive the motor at the right speed a tone is fed to the headphone socket (8) along with the audio signal. This happens in all positions of the main function switch when the motor is running.

HI FI PLAYBACK is the position used for high quality playback. *Warning: Do not accidentally turn the switch to* AUTOMATIC RECORD as already stated before. The meter, the line and headphone outputs are controlled by the line volume control. Usually the meter will indicate accurately (0dB on the scale = 320 NWb/M) when the line volume control is set to the zero on its scale. This can be checked by running a test tape.

The microphone is also live in this position and therefore the microphone volume control (2) should be kept turned down. If it is not and a microphone is connected then any sounds picked up by the microphone will be present at the line and headphone outputs. If on the other hand a microphone is not connected then the noise of the microphone pre-amplifier circuit will be fed to the outputs with a consequent reduction in the signal to noise ratio.

The Deck

The recorder will take tape reels of 7 inches diameter (18 cm) with the lid open and 5 inches (12.7 cm) with the lid closed. To load the tape onto the machine the deck function control (10) is turned to its most anti-clockwise position. This disengages the flutter filter rollers (20 & 21) and the pinch wheel assembly (13) and leaves a clear path between the feed and take up tension rollers (11 & 12). Thus tape can be fed from the feed spool on the feed spindle (22) round the feed tension roller (11) to the take up tension roller (12) onto the take-up spool on the take-up spindle (23) without any complicated twists and turns. Loading tape into the recorder is very simple. When the deck function control (10) is turned fully clockwise the tape is engaged with the magnetic heads and the capstan. As indicated before, the deck function control should be left in the position in which both dots coincide when the recorder is not being used. This ensures that the internal clutches and the pinchwheel are disengaged.

The accelerator button (19) applies full power to the motor by-passing the speed control and drives the tape at about 25ips on a set of new batteries. The speed can be increased by moving the deck function control to the position where the dots coincide. Take care not to turn it any further anti-clockwise since this will engage the rewind clutch.

The Tape Speed Selector (30) is situated on the left hand side of the recorder and has four positions. There are three speeds 15ips (38.1 cm/s), 7.5ips (19.05 cm/s) NAB and C.C.I.R., and 3.75ips (9.525 cm/s).

General Note

The Nagra III (and indeed the other Nagra tape recorders) is a good machine, well and logically made. It is not necessary to use force when operating it. If the operator feels that force is necessary then he is doing something wrong and should think again. If he does not think again he will break something.

Nagra III Connections

Microphone Input (9)

This is a Cannon XLR 3 male plug which follows the usual standard.

Pin 1 = Earth
Pin 2 = In Phase
Pin 3 = Neutral

The input is floating and symmetrical, there being no connection to earth. However some Nagra III's have been modified with a centre tap on the transformer being connected to earth. N.B: this input is out of phase with microphone pre-amplifiers (BS) and microphone mixers (BM) which are connected to the accessory socket.

Accessory Socket (27)

This is a DIN 6 pin female socket made by Tuchel. The pin connections are as follows:

Pin 2 = Earth. All voltages quoted are negative reference Earth.

Pin 1 = Directly connected to the negative terminal of the internal batteries. When rechargeable cells are used they can be charged through this connection. The charging device is designated PAR and takes 16 hours to fully recharge the batteries. It must not be used with ordinary dry cells. The PAR derives its power from a Nagra ATN power supply.

Pin 3 = Line input, affected by the line volume control, but with much greater sensitivity than the line input (26). This line input is the one used when the BS pre-amplifier and the BM mixer are used with a Nagra III. It is also the input used when a Sennheiser 04 type capacitor microphone is used.

Pin 4 = On models made before 1965 and designated NPH (sometimes NTPH) direct connection between this pin and earth or pin 2 switches off the motor of the recorder. I have found this to be very useful for editing tapes on the Nagra III, since it is possible to move the tape by hand without the motor

running but with the amplifiers on. *Warning:* by a strange freak of design connecting pin 4 to pin 2 on later Nagra III's designated **POH** and **PHO** the recorder will start to erase tape even though it is set in a playback mode. On these later models the function of pin 4 on the accessory socket is related to use of the machine with a playback synchroniser type SLO.

Pin 5 = Connected to the negative side of the EXT circuit. This is for powering the Nagra III from an external power source usually an ATN, which is a small transformer and rectifier. The voltage range that can be applied to this power input is between 11 and 24 volts.

Pin 6 = A stabilised power source at —10.5 volts. This is used to supply the power for the BM and BS amplifiers.

Pilot Tone Input (29)

To record pilot tone the following connections should be made.

Pins 2 & 3 = Earth. They should be strapped together.

Pin 1 = Pilot tone input.

Pin 6 = Clapper. The camera will send a signal which lies somewhere between +6 and +12 volts relative to earth (N.B: Positive with respect to earth) for the duration of the time when a small light in the gate is fogging the film, and this sets in action a 1KHz oscillator in the recorder which is recorded on the tape. This can only be heard off the tape and not in the direct mode. Thus the clapper tone cannot be used as a signal to the sound recordist to start recording.

Note on Designations for Nagra III

B = non pilot tone model

BH = non pilot tone model with built in loudspeaker.

NP = Pilot tone model

NPH = Pilot tone model with built in loudspeaker.

POH and PHO = Pilot tone models with built in loudspeakers built after 1965.

Appendix Two
The Nagra IV

A glance at the diagram will show immediately that the Nagra IV is considerably more complex than the Nagra III. Miniaturisation of electronic components has enabled the designers to compress facilities into a case the same size as that of the Nagra III that were carried outside the Nagra III. The following table will give an indication of the differences.

Facility	NAGRA IV	NAGRA III
second mic input	internal	external
Mic filters	internal	not available
Condensor mic ⎫	Plug in pre-amp	external
power supplies ⎭		
Radio slating receiver	plug in	external
frequency meter	plug in module	not available
Synchroniser	plug in module	external
Crystal pilot tone generator	plug in module	external

Surprisingly the ten-year period that elapsed between the two models did not make a very great difference in the recording quality. The range of facilities on the Nagra IV does however make it a very useful tape recorder.

There is a later model known as the Nagra IV-2. We will look at the differences between the two models in a note at the end of this appendix.

The Nagra IV that we examine will be the Pilot tone version. There are non pilot and much simpler versions available which have no bearing on film sound recording.

The Nagra IV L

There are two points of control, the main function switch (1) and the deck function control (40). Unlike the Nagra III there is no necessity to leave the deck function control in a neutral position since there is an interconnecting link from the main function switch which keeps the pinch wheel out of contact with the capstan. The deck function control extends beyond the confines of the deck in the rewind position and it is therefore not possible to close the lid of the recorder in this position. The main function switch has no BATT and EXT positions since this function is performed by a switch (9). It is normal when not using a Nagra IV to leave this switch in the External position, because the main function switch of the Nagra IV stands proud of the surface and can easily be knocked into an "on" position.

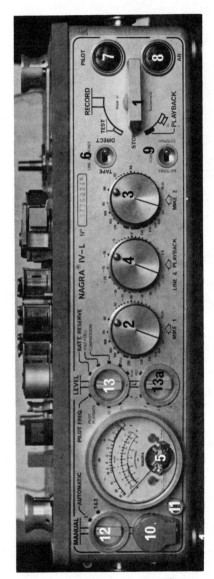

KEY:

1. Main Function Switch
2. Microphone No. 1 volume control
3. Microphone No. 2 volume control
4. Line and Playback volume control
5. Modulometer
6. Direct—tape switch
7. Pilot tone indicator.
8. AR Indicator
9. Battery/external power switch
10. Headphones monitoring socket
11. Headphones volume control
12. Microphone automatic volume control switch
13. Meter function switch
13a. Bass cut filter and reference tone switch.
14. Wireless slating aerial socket
15. Microphone input No. 2
16. Microphone input No. 1
17. Accessory socket
18. Line input
19. Mixer socket
20. Loudspeaker volume control
21. Loudspeaker
22. Power socket
23. Line output
24. Pilot tone input
25. External speed regulator socket
26. Speed selector
27. Feed spool spindle
28. Take up spool spindle
29. Feed spool tension roller
30. Takeup tension roller
31. Rewind/fast forward switch
32. Erase head
33. Record head
34. Pilot tone head
35. Replay head
36. Tape guide

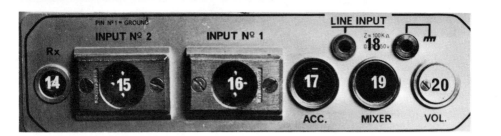

37. Flutter filter
38. Capstan
39. Pinchwheel assembly
40. Deck function control

N.B. 36, 37, 39, and 40 are also shown in their open position (Dotted).

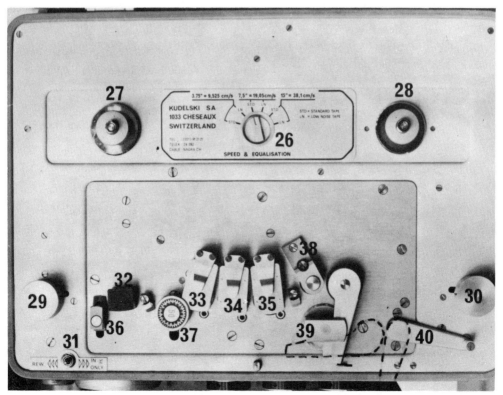

There are six positions of the main function switch:

HORIZONTAL—Off

TEST—This has the same function as the test position in the Nagra III. It enables the operator to listen to the sources of the sound, microphone or line, without actually recording. The Tape/Direct (6) switch must be in the DIRECT position since when it is in TAPE it is only possible to listen to signals from the tape at both the headphone monitoring socket (10) and the line output (23). If the recorder is receiving a pilot tone signal from an external source such as the mains or a camera, or from its own crystal generator, then the cross (7) will indicate. This is only true if the recorder has not got a QSLI replay synchroniser. With the QSLI pilot tone is only indicated when the machine is in the record mode.

FADE—The pitfall of the Nagra IV. This position of the main function switch was devised to eradicate the momentary run up period when the tape is not running at the right speed. If the switch is paused for a moment when switching from test to RECORD then the signal that reaches the tape is faded in rather than cut in. This is all very well, but has proved to be a trap for sound recordists who have trained themselves in using the Nagra III since the FADE position coincides with the HI-FI RECORD position. If the switch is left in the fade position the signal that reaches the tape is reduced in level by about 30dB. There are two indications that all is not well. The signal from the tape will be very low in level. This requires that the sound recordist switch to TAPE (6) immediately he starts recording. Secondly, the indicator marked AR (8), standing for All Right, does not appear as a cross until the recorder is functioning correctly, i.e. when it is left in the FADE position.

RECORD—The recorder operates as a normal recorder in this position.

PLAYBACK—In this position of the main Function Switch the tape recorder will replay the tape and a signal will be available at the headphone monitoring socket (10) and at the line output (23). The level of the signal will be as it was when the recording was made if the Tape/Direct switch (6) is in the TAPE position. If it is in the DIRECT position the line and playback volume control (4) must be used to adjust the level. This will be the same as the level in the TAPE position of the Tape/Direct switch when the volume control is set to 0. In this position of the volume control the meter will indicate accurately the level of the signal on the tape. The indication is $0 = 320$ nWb/M. In the DIRECT position of the switch the microphone inputs are also fed to the outputs.

PLAYBACK (LOUDSPEAKER)—The loudspeaker amplifier is switched on and sound can be heard from the loudspeaker (21) and the volume can be adjusted with the control (20). The sound from the loudspeaker can be heard regardless of the position of the tape direct switch (6). In this position the recorder can be run fast forward if the switch on the deck (31) is moved to the right. When the Nagra is fitted with a synchroniser, designated QSLI and which compares the frequency of the pilot tone on the tape with pilot tone from an external source such as the mains, a camera or the crystal, and adjusts the speed of the recorder's motor so that the two are the same (over a range of $\pm 3\%$), the recorder must be run in the PLAYBACK (LOUDSPEAKER) position of the main function switch for correct synchronisation. The Pilot tone indicator (7) will only show a cross when there are two sources of pilot tone present, i.e. from the tape and from the external reference. The amount of compensation to the speed being applied by the QSLI can be seen on the meter when its function switch (13) is set on SL.

That covers the functions of the main function switch. The deck function switch (40) has two positions, as illustrated in the diagram. In the rewind position the drive motor is connected to the feed spindle (27) but full power is only applied to the motor when the switch (31) is moved to the left. It is possible to rewind the tape in all positions of the main function switch except the OFF position, and when this is done in FADE or RECORD the bias oscillator is switched off to reduce the chance of accidental erasure. It is not worth taking the chance of rewinding in RECORD.

The Meter Function Switch: (13)

LEVEL—A peak reading meter for the signal strength: 0dB on the scale equals +8dBm equals 320nWb/M. It is safe to record to +4dB (520nWb/M) at which point a limiter built into the record circuit comes into action thus reducing the chances of distortion through over recording.

BATT. RESERVE—The strength of the batteries in comparison to the power needed by the recorder to keep the motor running at the correct speed. When this position of the switch is selected the AR indicator (8) goes off. The batteries are no longer worth using when the meter needle has fallen back to the left hand most side.

VOLT/CELL—The voltage of the batteries divided by 12 to give a value per cell. This can be a useful guide to the charge remaining in rechargeable cells.

COMPRESSION—The attenuation being applied to the signal from the microphones by the automatic level control amplifiers which can be brought into action for microphone number 1 or both mikes 1 and 2 by the automatic/manual switch (12). The circuit is a limiter compressor which has two recovery times, one rapid after short transient peaks, and one gradual according to the general level of the programme.

MOT—The current being used by the motor. If there is greater drag on the motor than there should be, the amount of current used will increase. A stage can be reached at which the motor control circuit will no longer be able to maintain the motor's correct running speed. At this point the needle of the meter will have just left the right hand end of the meter scale and the AR indicator (8) will go off.

BIAS—The meter indicates the strength of the bias signal.

PILOT FREQ.—Indicates the frequency deviation to ±4 percent of the pilot tone input to the recorder when the module QFM is installed. There are two versions available—QFM 50 and QFM 60 for 50- and 60Hz respectively. If the deviation in frequency exceeds 5 per cent the Pilot indicator (7) will go off as a warning to the sound recordist.

PILOT PLAYBACK—Operates when the QSLI module is inserted and indicates the strength of the pilot tone on the tape. The correct reading for a tape recorded on a Nagra IV should be about —2dB. Pilot tone recorded on a Nagra III is usually about 6dB greater.

SL—The deviation in speed being applied to the tape recorder's motor as a result of comparison between the pilot frequency from the tape and an external reference by the QSLI module.

RXμ—The strength of the signal from the radio receiver which can be built into the Nagra IV to receive signals from the Kudelski radio slating device. X—not connected.

Filter and Reference Generator Switch (13a)

This switch has 6 positions. The off position is the vertical one. Then there are 4 positions to the left marked from 1 to 4. These are bass cut positions of increasing severity and affect the two microphone inputs. There is one position to the right of the 'off' position which is a reference tone generator producing a —8dB (0dBm) 400Hz tone. The level of this tone is fixed.

Headphone Socket (10)

This is suitable for a standard Mono or unbalanced jack plug. The volume of the headphones can be adjusted with the volume control (11) which usually turns anti-clockwise for an increase in volume.

Pilot Indicator (7)

In the test and record modes the pilot indicator shows a cross when pilot tone is being fed to the recorder, either from a camera the mains or an internal crystal.

If a QSLI is fitted the indicator only works when pilot is being recorded; thus it does not indicate in the TEST position of the main function switch.

If a QFM frequency meter circuit is fitted the indicator only works if the frequency of the pilot tone lies within ±5%. Thus if 60Hz pilot tone is being recorded on a recorder fitted with a QFM50 the pilot indicator will not work.

In playback the indicator will only work if a QSLI is fitted and will indicate if pilot tone is present both from an external source and from tape.

AR Indicator (8)

This indicator shows up as a cross when everything connected to the recording process is in order. It will not indicate
(a) when the main function switch is in TEST and FADE.
(b) when the deck function selector is in the rewind position.
(c) in fast forward.
(d) when the meter function switch (13) is in BATT. RESERVE.
(e) when the battery supply is no longer adequate to run the motor at the correct speed.
(f) when there is some extra strain on the motor which prevents it from turning at the right speed.

Rewind/Fast Forward Switch (31)

This is a three position switch with 'off' in the centre. Rewind (selected on the deck function selector) will not work unless the switch is in the left hand position. Fast forward will only work when the main function switch (1) is in the PLAYBACK (LOUDSPEAKER) position.

Tape Speed Selector (26)

The Nagra IV has three speeds: 15ips (38.1cm/s), 7.5ips (19.05cm/s) and 3.75ips (9.525cm/s). There are two selector positions for each speed for standard and low noise tapes.

Nagra IV Plug Connections: Microphone Inputs (16 & 15)

These will accept Cannon XLR 3 11 plugs. Pin 1 = ground. The connections to the other pins depend on whether the recorder has been wired to the DIN or KUDELSKI standard.

DIN	KUDELSKI
Pin 2 = in phase	Pin 2 = neutral
Pin 3 = neutral	Pin 3 = in phase

There are two basic types of preamplifier that can be fitted into a Nagra IV: Type QPSE-200-XOYO for 200ohm dynamic microphones; QPSE-50-XOYO for 50ohm dynamic microphones and Type QPM-3-5 for Sennheiser capacitor microphones; the preamplifier supplies power to the mike.

NB. If the recorder is wired to the Kudelski standard then it is necessary to use a phase reversed microphone cable with the QPM-3-5 preamplifiers.

The Accessory Socket (17)

Similar to that used in the Nagra III but if the BM mixer is to be connected then it is advisable to insert QCB adaptor between the two. The only connections internally to this socket are

Pin 2 = ground
Pin 3 = line input
Pin 6 = —10volts stabilised (to provide power for accessories).

Mixer (19)

This socket has been provided· for a mixer which at the time of writing has not appeared. It is a 7 pin DIN standard socket with connections which can be useful to the ingenious Nagra user.

Pin 1 = fixed level input. 560mV equals 0dB on the meter.
Pin 2 = 50mA 10volt (—) stabilised power output.
Pin 3 = Direct signal output. 560mV into an impedance greater than 5Kohms equals 0dB on the meter.
Pin 4 = Unstabilised power output.
Pin 5 = Tape signal output. Similar to that at pin 3 in level.
Pin 6 = Connection of this pin to the —10volt pin (pin 2) stops the motor of the recorder. This can magnetise the heads of the recorder when used in the record position of the main function switch.
Pin 7 = Ground.

Power (22) and Pilot (24) Sockets

The functions of the pins of these two sockets are clearly shown on the side of the Nagra. The ATN mains power supply is plugged into the power socket.

When the Nagra has an internal crystal pilot tone generator the tone output is at the pin marked XTAL. A small plug is available which can be used to connect this pin with the pilot tone input.

Speed (25)

A circuit called a QSV speed varier can be connected to the speed control circuit in the Nagra and can be used to alter the speed by ±11%. This is useful when for instance the QSLI circuit is unable to synchronise a pilot tone

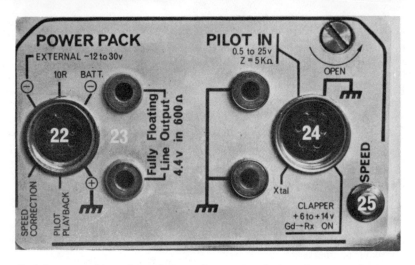

recording because either the reference frequency of the pilot tone frequency on the tape are outside the ±3% limit.

Differences Between the Nagra IVL and the Nagra 4.2L

Main Function Switch(1)

The fade position has been removed and the option to record without the built-in limiter added, as can be seen from the photograph.

The Tape/Direct Switch (6)

In the TEST position of the main function switch (1) the monitoring output of the recorder is connected to the DIRECT Circuit even if the switch is in the TAPE position.

Meter Tape/Direct Switch (41)

On the 4.2L it is possible to switch the meter to the tape position also. The switch is spring loaded in the DIRECT position.

The Bass Cut Switch (7)

This switch is devoted to filtering on the microphone inputs only.

The Reference Tone Switch (42)

The small button between and below the Line and Playback and the second microphone volume controls feeds reference tone to the tape when pressed.

On the first models of the 4.2L the oscillator produced a square wave signal. This was to facilitate emergency azimuth adjustments on location, since the high frequency content of the square wave enables quite accurate adjustments to be made by ear. However, in order to get a reference tone that will replay —8dB on the Nagra meter (0dBm) it is necessary to record the signal at —10dB on the meter. This created confusion and the oscillator on later models produces a mixed tone ($\pm$1KHz $+$10KHz) with which it is still possible to adjust azimuth by ear but which records and replays at —8dB on the meter.

The Speed Socket (25)

The Variateur de Vitesse is different and therefore has been supplied with a different plug so that no mistake can be made. The speed can be varied by $\pm$12%.

Appendix Three

The Nagra IS

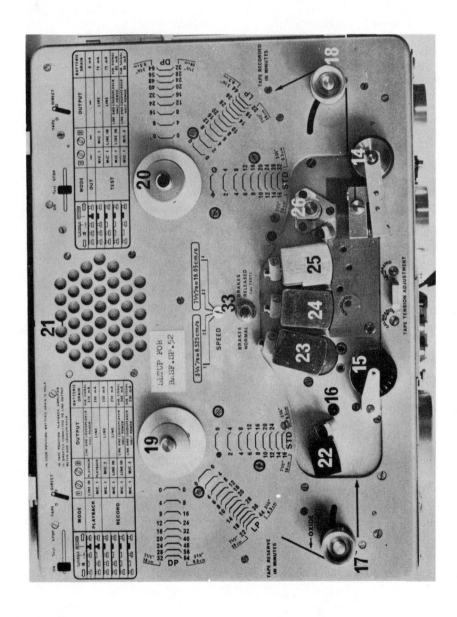

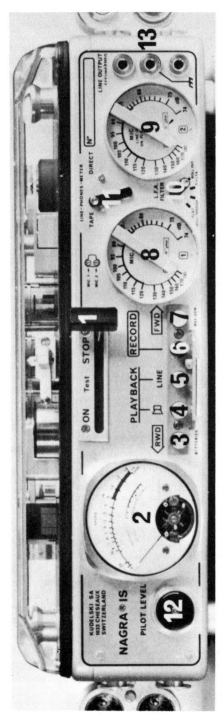

KEY:
1. Main Function Switch
2. Meter
3. Rewind, Battery meter and Frequency tester selector
4. Playback (loudspeaker) selector
5. Line selector (Playback and Record)
6. Record selector
7. Fast forward and reference tone selector
8. Microphone number one volume control
9. Microphone number two, line and playback volume control
10. Bass cut switch
11. Meter, line and headphone TAPE/DIRECT switch
12. Pilot indicator (record and replay)
13. Balanced Line output
14. Pinchwheel assembly
15. Flutter filter and strobe
16. Pilot tone strobe light
17. Feed spool tension roller
18. Take up spool tension roller
19. Feed spool spindle
20. Take up spool spindle
21. Loudspeaker
22. Erase head
23. Record head
24. Pilot tone head
25. Replay head
26. Capstan
27. Microphone input number one
28. Microphone input number two
29. Headphone output
30. Pilot tone socket
31. Accessory socket
32. Line input
33. Edit brake release

Description

IS stands for Idiot System. The IS is supposed to be virtually foolproof, very easy to operate. Needless to say, it crams a considerable number of facilities into its casing which is smaller than that of the Nagra III and IV. It is a lightweight recorder which falls somewhere in between the III and the IV in sophistication.

In describing the function of the recorder it is necessary to examine the controls (1), (3), (4), (5), (6), and (7) in the diagram together: *the Main Function Switch (1), Rewind, Battery Meter, & Frequency Tester Selector (3), Playback (Loudspeaker) Selector (4), Line Selector (Playback and Record) (5), Record Selector (6), Fast Forward and Reference Tone Selector (7).*

The three centre buttons, Loudspeaker (4), Line (5), and Record (6) are connected so that when one is pressed any other that is in will jump out. When they are all out the recorder is OFF. Gentle pressure on a button which is out will achieve this status. Depressing one of these buttons is necessary before the recorder will work, but the current drained from the batteries is minimal until the Main Function Switch (1) is moved to either TEST or ON. The buttons do what they say; but there is an exception. The RECORD button (6) switches the recorder into the record mode with both microphone inputs (27 & 28) active and controlled by volume controls 8 and 9 respectively. If the Line Selector (5) is depressed at the same time so that both the record button (6) and the line selector (5) are both in then the volume control (9) marked Mic 2, line input or playback is connected to the line input (the mike input being disconnected). If the Playback (Loudspeaker) Selector (4) is also depressed then the loudspeaker is activated at half its usual strength.

Let us remain with the record mode for the moment. When the record button is depressed and the main function switch (1) is set on TEST it is possible to listen to the signal arriving at the recorder through the microphone inputs (27 and 28) by plugging headphones (ideally with an impedance of 50 ohms) into the monitoring socket (29). The signal at this socket in TEST is unaffected by the TAPE/DIRECT switch (11). The meter indicates the strength of the signal being fed to the record amplifier, and like the monitoring socket is unaffected by the TAPE/DIRECT switch (11). The signal is also fed to the line output (13—also unaffected by the TAPE/DIRECT switch). If pilot tone is being fed to the pilot tone amplifier from an external source such as a camera or the mains, or from the internal crystal oscillator via a shorting link in the pilot tone input (30) then the pilot tone indicator (12) will show a white patch (normally black). By pressing in the button marked RWD and Batt (3) the meter will indicate the strength of the batteries on the scale marked BATTERIES Volts/Cell and will illuminate a light emitting diode (16) which I have called the pilot tone strobe light. Pulling out the button (3) has the same effect on the pilot tone strobe light (16) but not on the meter. This light emitting diode will only illuminate when pilot tone is being fed into the recorder. It can be used in conjunction with the flutter filter and strobe (15) to check the speed of the tape and the frequency of pilot tone (of which more later). The button marked FWD Ref (7) provides reference tone when the record selector (6) is in use. When the main function switch (1) is in TEST reference tone can be obtained when the button (7) is pulled out, but when the main function switch is in ON reference tone can only be obtained by pushing the FWD Ref selector (7) in (against a spring).

When the main function switch is moved to the ON position the Pinch Wheel (14) is engaged with the capstan (26) and the flutter filter and strobe wheel (15) is rotated so that the tape is engaged with the erase head (22), the record head (23), the pilot tone head (24) and the replay head (25) and the motor is switched on, and the recorder begins to record. If the direct/tape switch (11) is switched to the tape position then the monitoring output for headphones (29), the line output (13) and the meter (2) all derive their signal from the replay head (25) and its associated amplifiers.

The RWD (3) and FWD (7) fast rewind and fast forward buttons do not work when the record Selector (6) is depressed. The playback (loudspeaker) (4) & playback line (5) selectors have little difference in function except that the first adds the loudspeaker to the replay circuit. The level of the signal at the headphone socket (29), line output (13) and the loudspeaker (21) is fixed when the direct/tape switch (11) is set on TAPE. The meter (2) indicates the strength of signal on playback which will be the same as that during the time when the recording was made providing the recorder is set up correctly for the tape being used.

When the tape/direct switch (11) is in the DIRECT position the level of the signal at the outputs (29 and 13), the loudspeaker (21), and, consequently, the indication on the meter (2), are all controlled by the line volume control (9).

To wind the tape fast in either direction the main function switch (1) must be in TEST or STOP. All that is required is to push RWD (3) or FWD (7) briefly. Pushing the same selector again stops the fast winding process. In the TEST position of the main function switch (1) the tape is held in contact with the heads, and although the pressure is not great will obviously increase the wear on the heads rapidly. It is however useful for locating sounds on the tape; the volume is controlled by the line and playback volume control (9) regardless of the position of the direct/tape Switch (11). The tape should be stopped before moving the main function switch (1) to the ON position, although there is a safety circuit which switches out the winding motors if this is done.

In the TEST position of the main function switch (1) it is possible to use the recorder for editing tape. The brakes which work on the feed and take up spindles (19 and 20) can be switched out of action by the edit brake release (33). The volume of the signal heard either from the loudspeaker (21) or the headphones (29) is controlled by the Line volume control (9), regardless of the position of the direct/tape Switch (11).

Whenever pilot tone on the tape is being replayed the pilot tone indicator will show its white flag. The light emitting diode (16) is driven by the pilot tone on the tape when the recorder is in the replay mode and consequently strobes with the flutter filter and strobe wheel (15) giving an indication of the frequency of the pilot tone versus the speed of the tape. It is appropriate here to point out how the pilot tone strobe light (16) and the flutter filter and strobe can be used for testing the frequency of pilot tone or the accuracy of the speed of the tape. Any calculations using the strobe must be approximate, since the system to be described is dependant on the diameter of the flutter filter and strobe wheel which will vary slightly with temperature, tape slip relative to the flutter filter and strobe wheel (15), and the speed of the tape. In the 50Hz version there is one strobe bar per cycle; thus if the strobe moves through one bar per second there is a frequency shift of 2 percent (or 1Hz) and 1 bar in 10 seconds = .29. Any innacuracies in the system can be calibrated by recording a piece of tape using the built in crystal oscillator as a reference. Thus it is possible to calculate whether the tape is running fast or slow and by how much. (Bars moving clockwise by 1 bar in 5 seconds = 0.4% fast (multiply no. bars/sec. by 2 for %.) This can be rechecked on replay and confirmed. To check the frequency of pilot tone on a previously recorded tape the assumption has to be made that the tape recorder will run at approximately the same speed a minute or two after calibration. The tape is played and the strobe bars counted. If the bars move fast anti-clockwise, say 18 bars in 10 seconds, then the frequency of the pilot tone on the tape is far too high, by 3.6%. Add to this the previously

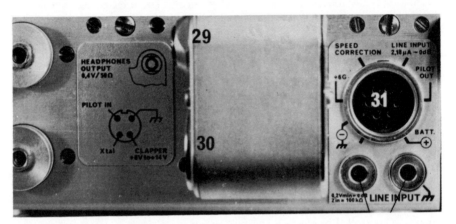

calculated .4% discrepancy in the speed of the recorder and you get a total difference of 4%. This could easily be the difference between running at 24- and 25fps. The way to check the frequency of the pilot tone from a camera and consequently the speed of the camera is as follows. Calibrate the tape recorder with the crystal as described above. Record some tape deriving the pilot tone from the camera. If the strobe moves clockwise the frequency of the pilot tone is lower than that of the crystal and vice versa. The formula is the same: % frequency deviation = No. bars/sec x 2. Clockwise movement of the strobe means the frequency of the pilot tone being checked (from tape or an external source) is low in comparison to the crystal. I must stress again that the system must be inaccurate, but it is good enough for checking for major faults in the speed of a camera or the frequency of pilot tone.

When purchasing the recorder it is necessary to specify the frequency at which it will be used most, i.e. 50 or 60Hz.

The Bass Cut Switch (10)

This is effective in record and replay. It affects both microphone and line inputs. It even affects the level of the reference tone in the position S + LFA. The graph shows how it affects the frequency response of the recorder.

The pin connections for the accessory socket (31) are visible in the photograph.

200

Appendix Four

The Nagra SN

KEY:
1. Main Function lever
2. Meter
3. Input plug
4. Pilot tone and remote plug
5. Output
6. Automatic level control threshold control
7. Main function switch safety catch
8. Feed spindle
9. Take up spindle
10. Rewind handle
11. Rewind handle release
12. Speed control
13. Battery test
14. Rear casing locking screws

Description

SN stands for Small Nagra. The recorder was originally designed for spy operations. It is extremely compact and light in weight—1¼ lbs (½ a kilo), and capable of very high quality recording. It has been adapted for film recording, it being possible to record a synchronising signal from a crystal oscillator.

Mechanical functions and the on/off switch are controlled by the main function lever (1). There is a safety catch for this lever located (7) near the meter. The recorder is always in replay when it is switched on but whether it is in record is determined by whether or not anything is plugged into the input plug (3).

To record: Plug the microphone into the socket (3) and press the main function lever (1) in towards the body of the recorder. If it will not move then check that the safety catch (7) is released. There is a built in compressor which controls the recording level, but it is possible to adjust the threshold of this with the control at 6. The meter indicates the amount of attenuation being applied by the compressor. There are two speeds controlled by the screwdriver operated switch (12) between the take-up spindle (9) and the rewind handle (10). The high speed (indicated by the red dot) is 3.75 ips (9.525cm/s) and the slow speed 1.875 ips (4.7625cm/s). The spools of 0.15inch (3.81mm) tape run for 27 minutes at the high speed (providing the standard tape is used—long play and double play are available but not recommended for the highest possible standard). There is no TEST position for the recorder so it is necessary to run tape to find out about microphone positioning, ALC threshold, and sound quality. The monitoring is done in the TAPE mode by plugging headphones of less than 1 Kohm impedance into the output socket (5). This needs a miniature jack plug.

To rewind the tape the main function lever is pulled out and locked by engaging the slot in the lever with the casing of the recorder. The process of rewinding is done by hand and therefore it is necessary to release the rewind handle (10) by pressing the release button (11). Long fingernails are necessary to lift the shiny handle crank, and sometimes the whole assembly will not click into position above the level of the spools. When this last happens turn the feed spool slightly. To rewind turn the handle clockwise. When the rewinding is complete the rewind handle is lined up with the space between the spools and gently pushed back into its resting space between the spools (the main function lever REWIND position is used for loading tape into the recorder.) *Before the tape is replayed unplug the input plug* otherwise the recorder will be in the record mode and will erase the recording. The SN's batteries (2 x penlight batteries) are fitted into the recorder by removing the rear casing by unscrewing the locking screws (14) half a turn. They last about 5½ hours providing high quality cells are used.

As can be seen from the diagram it is possible to plug in various accessories such as a remote control, synchronising input, and speed controller.

Above: *Nagra SN, showing the recorder set for rewinding the tape.* Below: *Nagra SN with the back cover removed, revealing the printed circuit boards, the motor and, at the top of the picture the two penlight cells needed for power.*

Appendix Five

Interlock Systems

There are two basic methods for locking film machines together in synchronism (so that they all run at the same speed or rate frame for frame both forwards and backwards).

Mechanical Interlock

As implied the machines are coupled mechanically to one set of gears or shafts so that when one machine turns so do all the others, and they may indeed be run by a common motor. The method is simple but has the disadvantage that the machines have to be close together, including, in a dubbing theatre, the projector. It is not possible to run separate machines independently.

A Selsyn generator of the type used in a dubbing theatre.

Electrical Interlock

Several types exist of which the commonest are:

(a) SELSYN, standing for self synchronous. In this system a master motor-generator generates a three-phase alternating magnetic field. The slave motors, which drive the film recorder, dubbers, projector and footage counter, are supplied with the same alternating current which creates the magnetic field in the master motor. Thus an alternating current is generated in the coils of the rotors of the motors. When the rotor of the master motor is turned, the alternating magnetic fields in the slaves rotate in sympathy and the slaves' rotors follow. Thus one revolution of the master motor is duplicated by one revolution of the rotors in each of the slaves.

The advantages of the system are that the pieces of equipment can be in separate places and need only be connected by wires. A separate synchronous motor in tandem with, or indeed part of, a selsyn motor enables the equipment to be run independently.

In a variation of the selsyn system the main drive can come from these synchronous motors, the selsyn part only being used during the periods of running up to and down from running speed. This latter system tends to be a bit rough in its action and can cause torn perforations and lost loops in film sound reproducers and recorders.

(b) SYNCHROSTART, a system developed by Perfectone, uses only synchronous motors. There is a generator which generates a three-phase supply which can be varied in frequency from zero to the normal supply frequency. To run up to speed, the equipment is locked together with three-phase direct current (i.e. zero frequency) which is slowly converted into an alternating current. When the line frequency is reached the generator switches over to the main supply, and the motors run in synchronism. The reverse process is applied to stop the equipment in lock. The advantages over a selsyn system are that only synchronous motors are needed in the equipment, and they can run at any synchronous speed. Thus each motor can be run independently of the interlock mechanism. The system is expensive.

Appendix Six

Filming to Playback

When filming to playback it is necessary to have a tape which has been prepared with the correct pilot tone signal. A preproduction meeting with the cameraman and the editor of the film is not a bad idea. At this meeting it should be determined whether the film is to be shot at 24 or 25 frames per second. There are two definite reasons for shooting at 25fps: exhibition on television and availability of of equipment.

When the decision has been taken the sound which is to be used for the playback should be tranferred to film at the required speed and to tape with pilot tone. This pilot tone tape must be made at the same time or copied from the film. At all transfer stages the same frequency that is being used to drive the film must be used to record the pilot tone. It is a good idea to make at least two copies of the pilot tone tape since in its use in the field it could become damaged by over use.

The sound recordist is then armed with the essentials for playback: the pilot tone replay tape, and the knowledge that the editor, the cameraman and he himself all know the speed at which the filming is to take place. There are a few other points; for instance if the action is to start immediately the sound (let us suppose it to be music) starts then the actors who are going to do the miming to the sound must have some kind of cue. The general thing is to record a series of three pips on the tape immediately before the music. If these have not been recorded on the tape already and if they are needed in a hurry then there are two ways to cope:

(1) Mark the first note of music on the tape. Turn the tape over so that the take up spool becomes the feed spool etc, and the tape is *running backwards* in the tape recorder. In this way it is possible to record on the tape with the certain knowledge that there is no chance of erasing some of the audio. Run the recorder in record holding the pinch wheel away from the capstan. When absolutely ready let go and with the oscillator built into the recorder record three pips about a second apart from each other. This has the disadvantage that there is no guarantee that the new pilot tone track will match the old one both in frequency or phase with the result that there may be a momentary change in the speed of the replay tape recorder as it finds the correct speed to run at.

(2) If a recorder is available to record guide tracks then make a pilot tone copy using the one recorder to replay in sync with the mains while doing a transfer to the other recording the pilot tone from the mains.

The recordist should have some extra equipment with him for replay.

(1) Amplifiers and loudspeakers are no good unless they can be heard. The type marketed by Nagra designated DH is adequate for most jobs. It runs off 12 batteries and provides a loud 6 watts of sound. The quality is not tremendous but certainly audible. But, for pop groups 6 watts is never enough. They will always ask for more, and the only solution is to try to arrange to plug into their own public address system. This is usually a massive several hundred watts and is adequately deafening.

SYNCHRONOUS PLAYBACK

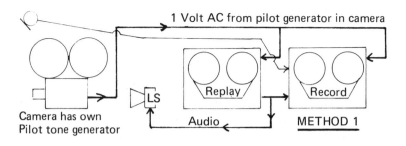

1 Volt AC from pilot generator in camera

Camera has own
Pilot tone generator

Replay

Record

Audio

METHOD 1

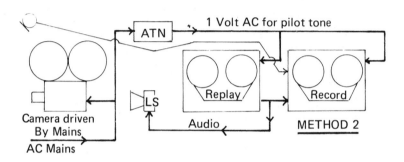

1 Volt AC for pilot tone

ATN

Camera driven
By Mains
AC Mains

Replay

Record

Audio

METHOD 2

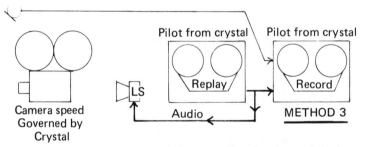

Pilot from crystal   Pilot from crystal

Camera speed
Governed by
Crystal

Replay

Record

Audio

METHOD 3

The Microphone in each method is for recording the clapper board.

*The three most used systems for synchronous playback. If it is not necessary
to record a guide track the right-hand recorder can be left out in each case.*

The sound recordist therefore needs either a DH or similar amp/speaker,
a lead to connect to the playback machine (and the one supplied is usually not
long enough), and, if the pop group's own PA is to be used, a selection of
plugs and a soldering iron (the standard mono jack plug is usually what is
needed).

(2) Some easily seen system for marking the tape is needed. I like to use

joining tape and a black spirit-based marker since the white tape is easily seen under low lighting conditions, and the marker does not leave a deposit in the same way as a wax or chinagraph pencil does. The sound recordist therefore needs a splicing block, some joining tape and a razor blade, and a black indelible marker, or a chinagraph pencil (deprecated).

(3) If the sound to be played back is music with vocals, then try to get a transcript of the words. I cannot begin to say how helpful this can be.

(4) If system 4 (see diagram) is to be used to record the guide track, then some kind of splitter for the pilot tone feed is necessary. There are two ways. Make up a splitter or if cannon microphone extension leads are used then a microphone splitter can be used.

(5) Sometimes, to save money, a wild camera is used for filming. This simply means that there is no blimp around the camera and that it is cheaper to hire. It will still have some way of running synchronously. The problem that arises is that as a result of the noise that the mechanism makes the camera operator cannot hear the playback. It may be necessary for him to hear since some camera movements may rely on sound for their motivation. A headphone extension should therefore be taken along as well, and, since sometimes the focus puller also needs to hear, a splitter and a second pair of cans.

For replay the person who is operating the recorder must be quick at working with tape. It is sometimes necessary to find and mark up a new cue very quickly and accurately. It helps to mark the beginning of each verse before the shooting starts and to mark up these points on the transcript.

Inevitably, when using a Nagra IV, the moment will come when one starts a playback in the fast mode. This can be avoided by having a rubber band around the switch and attached to the left-hand carrying strap knob, so that the switch is always pulled to the fast rewind position.

A Nagra 4.2L being used for synchronous playback. Because the main function switch has to be used in the Loudspeaker Playback position to obtain sync, and since this coincides with the fast function, a rubber band attached to the switch on the deck prevents accidents.

Index

Acoustic labyrinth, 39-40
Alternating current, 21
Amplitude, 16
Amps, 21-23
Atmosphere track, 175
Attenuators, 84-85
Azimuth, 56-58
Azimuth track (optical), 164

Balanced line, 42, 44
Bel, 17
Bias, 54-56, 60
Buzz track, 164, 175

Capacitance, 24
Capacitors, 24
Click track, 162
Compatibility, 31-32
Cross-mod test, 170
Crystal sync, 107
Crystamatic, 112

Dashpot, 91
Decibel, 16, 18
Direct current, 21
Distortion, 30-31
Dolby system, 163-64, 168
Double system sound recording, 96, electrical synchronisation, 96; mechanical synchronisation, 96
Drop out, 54, 56
Dubbing, 130-47
Dubbing theatre, 130, 133-47
Dynamic range, 18

Ear, 9
Echo, 145-47
Editing, 124-26, equipment, 124-26
Eigen tones, 19
Electret, 72
Electrostatic charge, 24
Eustachian tube, 9

Faders, 134; quadrant, 134; rotary, 134; slide, 134
Farads, 24
Film reproducer, 130, 133
Filters, 135-39; high pass, 136-39; low pass, 136-39; telephone, 140-43; variable band stop, 136-39
Fish pole, 171-73
Fleming's right-hand/left-hand rule, 25
Fletcher/Munsen curves, 17
Frequency, 12-14
Frequency response, 31, 59, 163-65

Graphic equaliser, 136-39

Harmonics, 13-16

Head degausser, 57
Headphones, 64
Hertz, 12
Huygen's principle, 19

Impedance, 26, 32
Inductance, 24-25
Induction, 25, 60
Interlock, 133-35

Leaders, 152-53
Light valve, 164, 166, 170
Loop-box, 142
Loops, 142-44, 161

Magnetic film recorder, 91, 94, 97-101, 121-23, 130-47
meters, 54, 58, 63-64
Microphones, 30-45, 69-86, condenser, 35; general properties, 30; handling, 171-76; moving coil, 35; ribbon, 35
Microphone pre-amplifier, 66-69
Mirror galvanometer, 164, 166, 170
Mixers, 87, 135-39
Multi-camera set ups, 115
Multimeters, 27

Neo-Pilot tone, 102
Nodal points, 16

Ohms, 23
Ohm's Law, 23
Optical sound, 163-68; cameras, 168; reproduction, 163-68
Oscillator, 27-29, 54, 57, 107, 121
Oscilloscope, 27-29, 101, 121

Patch panel, 121, 133
Perfectone, 103
Perforation pitch, 150
Permeability, 51
Pilot tone, 99, 101-07, 114
Pitch, 13-15
Polar diagrams, 32, 34
Post-synchronisation, 143-45, 160
Projector, 130-34
Proximity effect, 39

Radio slating, 109
Ranger tone, 103
Reference tone, 117, 120
Resistance, 23
Rock and roll, 130, 140

Selsync, 132
Shielding, 41-42
Signal, 19
Signal-to-noise ratio, 19, 31, 163
Silent turn over, 106

Sine waves, 12
Single-system sound recording, 94-97
Sound blankets, 175
Sound effects (FX), 129, 159-61
Sound perspective, 174-75
Sound waves, 9-12
Spacing, 150-52
Speed of sound, 12
Splicing block, 124, 126
Sync mark, 151-53
Sync plop, 154-55, 161
Synchronisation, 90
Synchronism, 130
Synchro-pulse, 98, 103
Synchrotone, 103

Tachometer head, 57
Tape joiner (film), 148-50
Tape recorders, 46-70; amplifier and meter,
circuits, 60; cassette, 48; controls, 51;
open reel, 48; tape deck, 49; tape trans-
port, 48
Test tapes, 56-57
Threshold of hearing, 17
Threshold of pain, 17
Track-laying, 151-55, 159
Transducers, 10, 30
Transfer, 117-22

Unbalanced line, 42

Variable area sound track, 163, 166
Variable density sound track, 163
Voltmeter, 28-29, 121
Volts, 21, 23
Volume controls, 133-34

Watts, 23
Wavelength, 12-13, 15-16